Rachel Feinstein

Secrets

GAGOSIAN

Beverly Hills

Granite Bay

2018
Inkjet print and UV semigloss liquid laminate on wallpaper
Dimensions variable

Rêve de Bonheur
2018
Oil and enamel on mirror
42 × 54 inches (106.7 × 137.2 cm)

Corine

2018
Majolica
51 ¼ × 37 ⅜ × 49 ¼ inches (130.2 × 95 × 125 cm)

Shadow Mountain Drive
2018
Oil and enamel on mirror
42 × 54 inches (106.7 × 137.2 cm)

The Lake House
2018
Oil and enamel on mirror
42 × 54 inches (106.7 × 137.2 cm)

Bradbury
2018
Oil and enamel on mirror
42 × 54 inches (106.7 × 137.2 cm)

𝔖𝔲𝔫𝔰𝔢𝔱 𝔅𝔩𝔳𝔡.
2018
Oil and enamel on mirror
42 × 54 inches (106.7 × 137.2 cm)

Scènes de Jardins

2018
Oil and enamel on mirror
48 × 106 inches (121.9 × 269.2 cm)

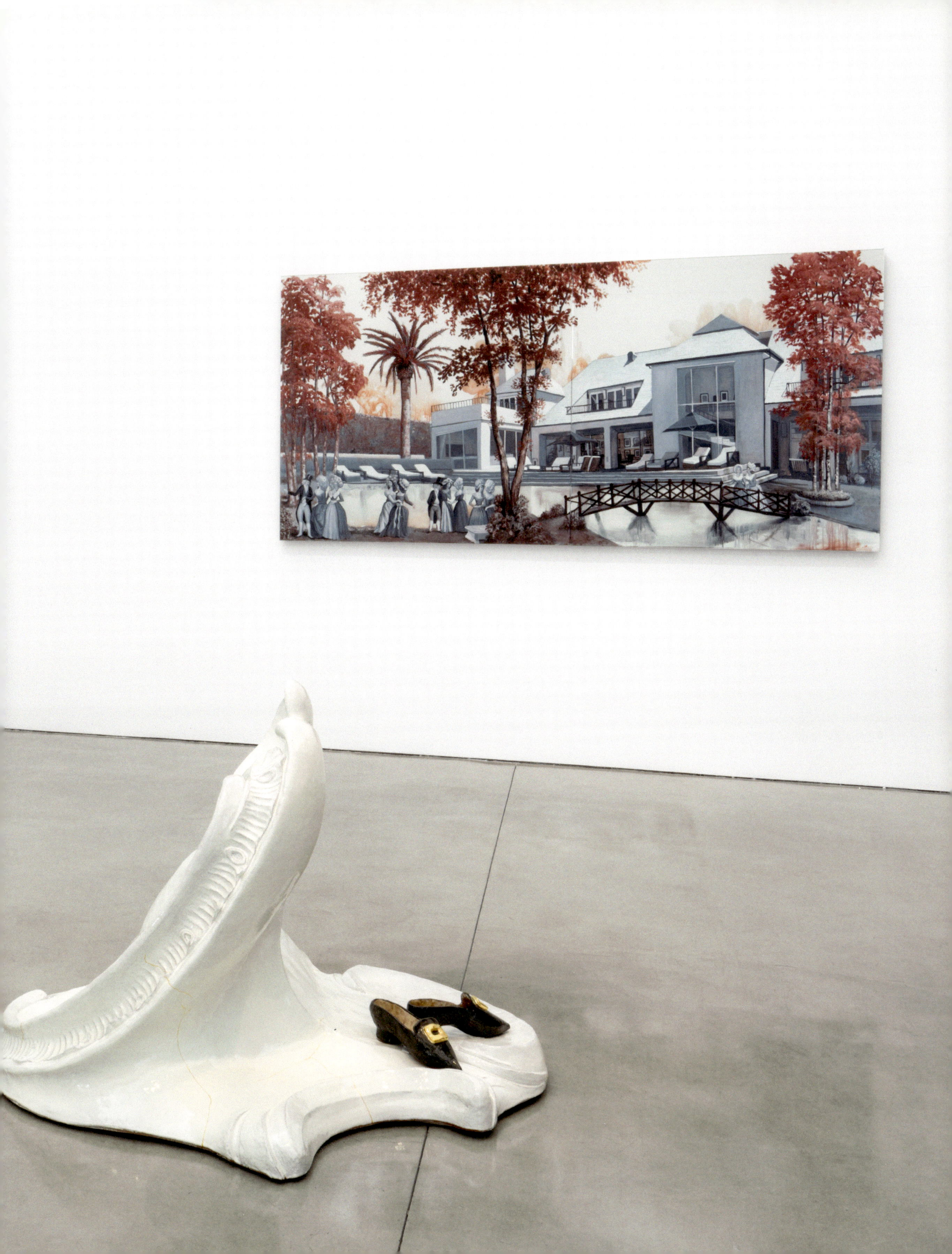

Octavio
2018
Majolica
39 ½ × 53 ½ × 43 ⅜ inches (100.3 × 135.9 × 110.2 cm)

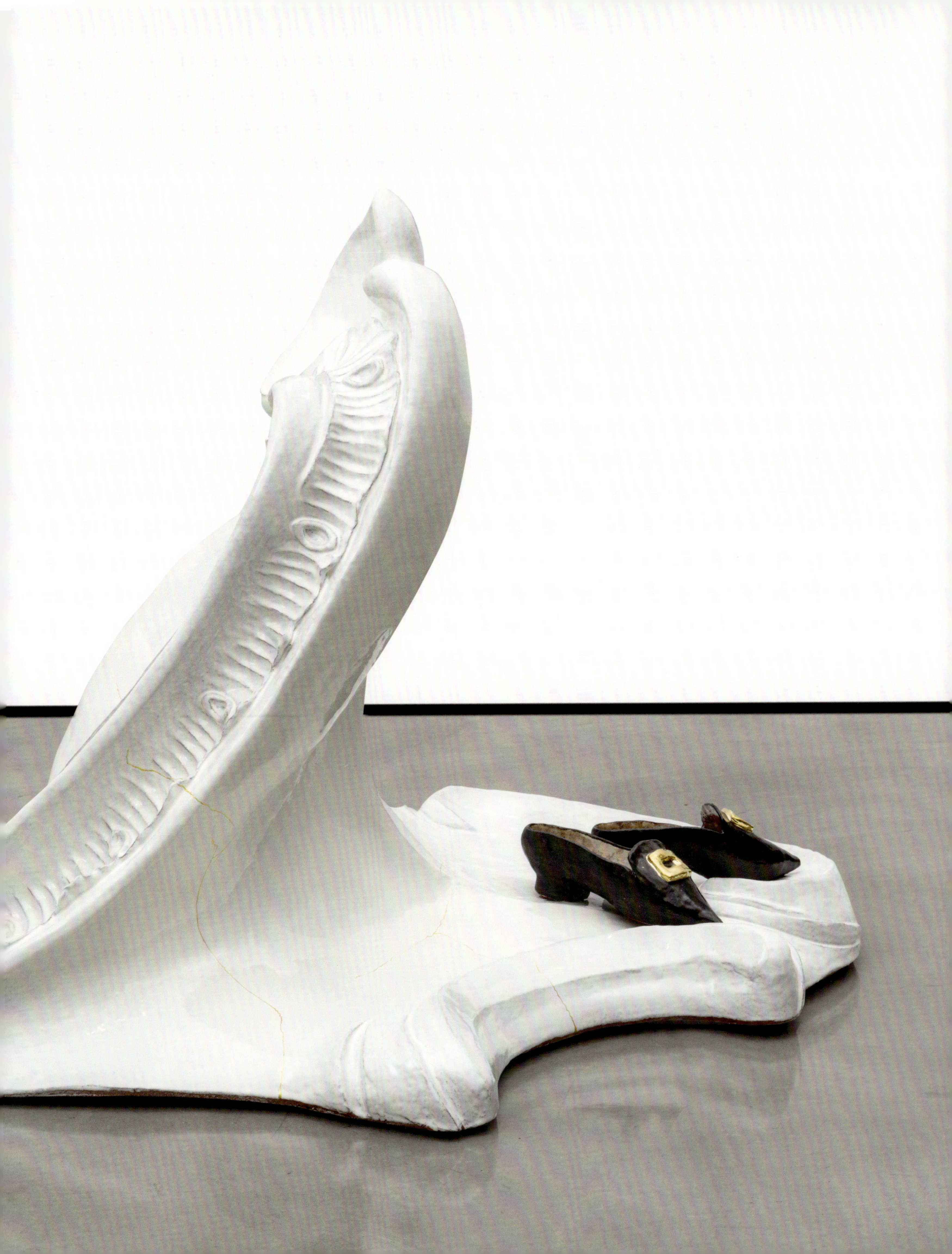

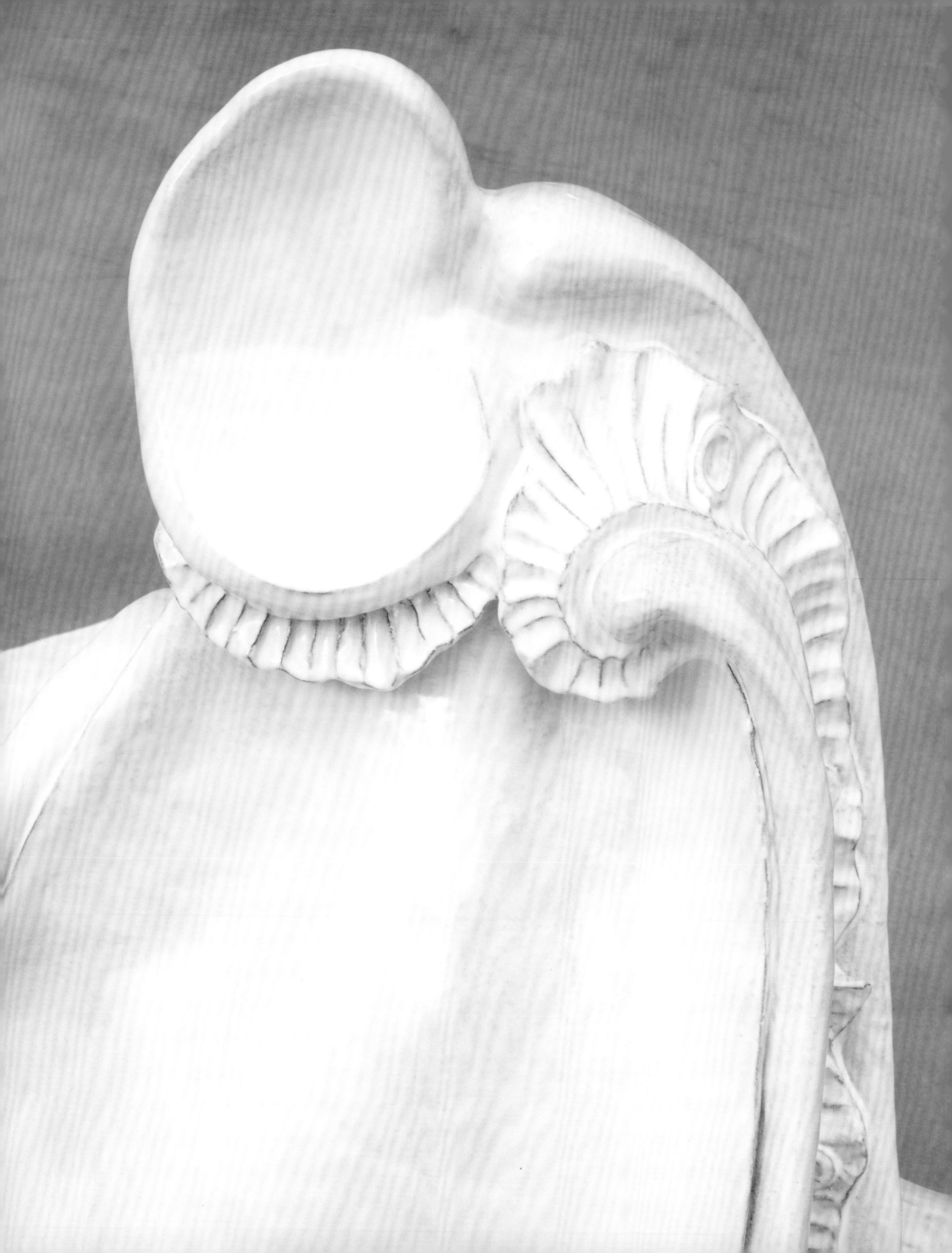

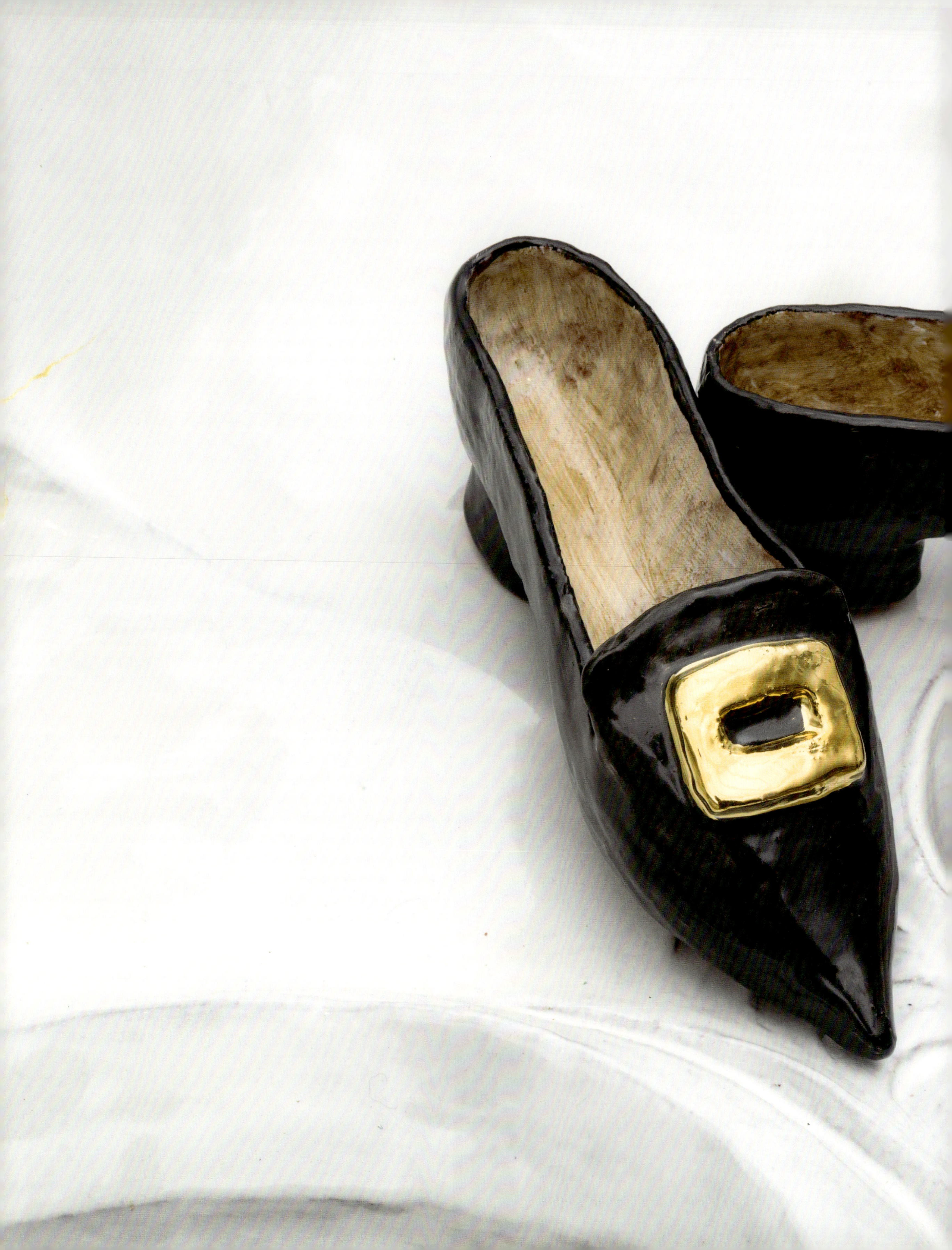

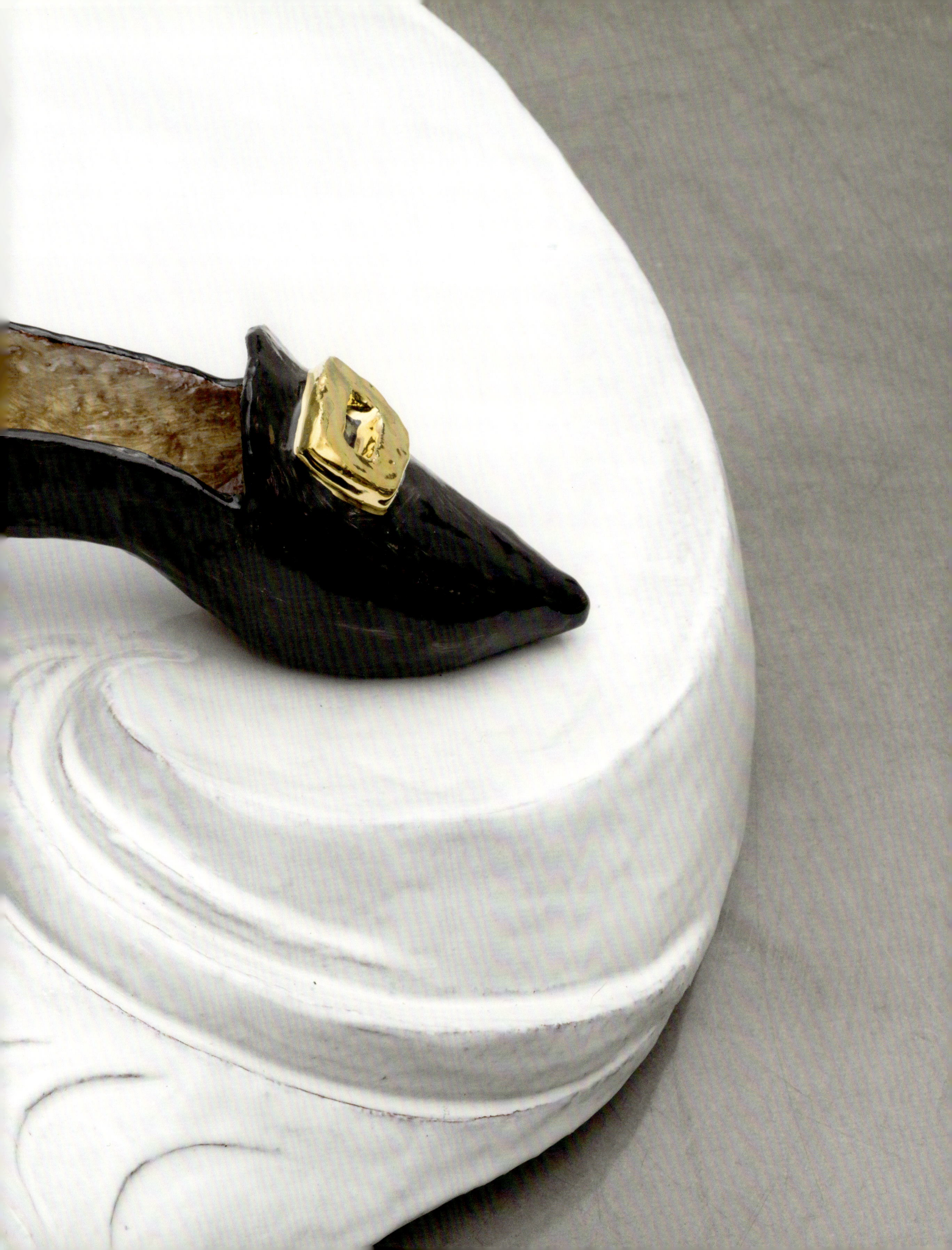

Silver Lake Blvd.

2018
Oil and enamel on mirror
25 × 32 inches (63.5 × 81.3 cm)

Neutra Place
2018
Oil and enamel on mirror
25 × 32 inches (63.5 × 81.3 cm)

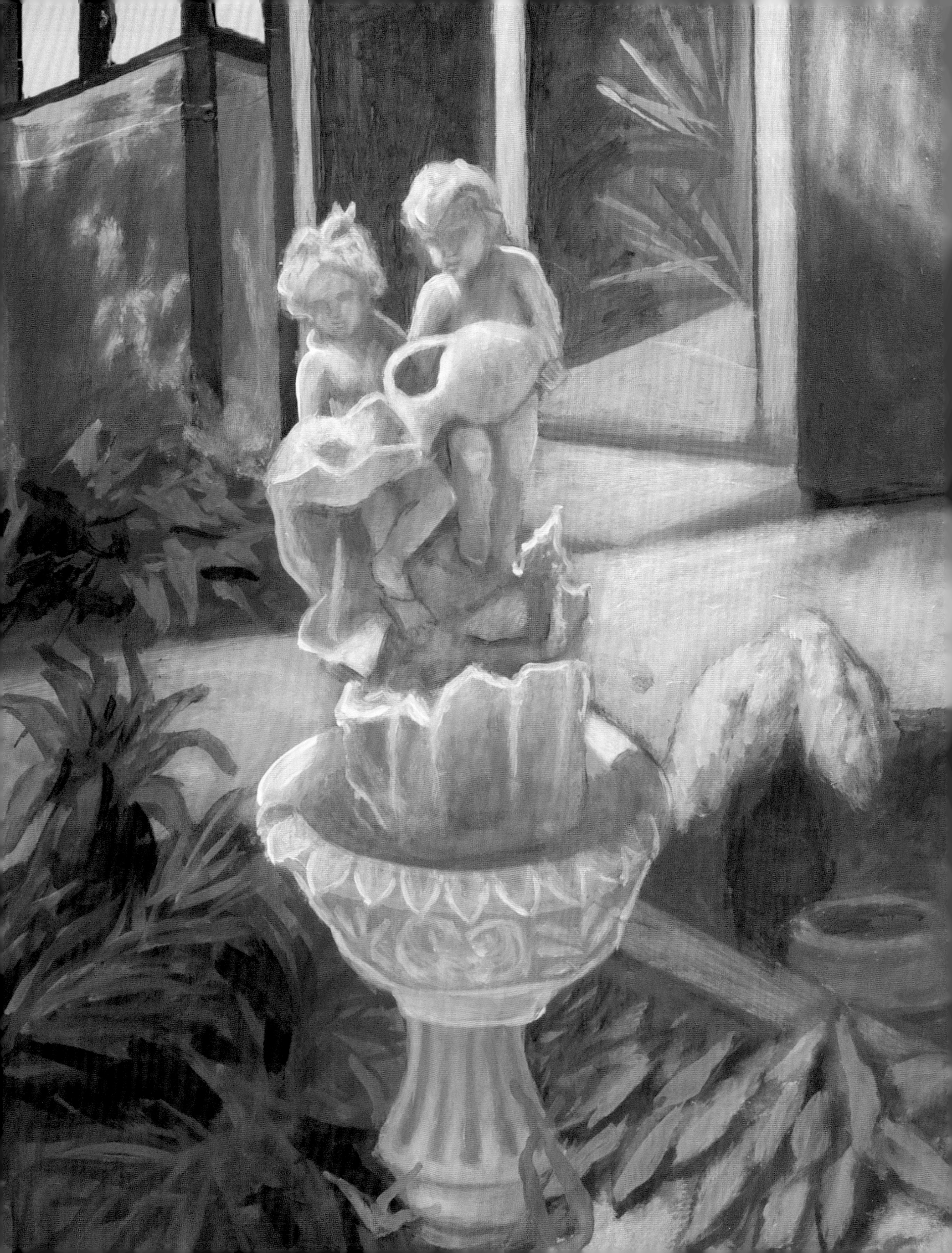

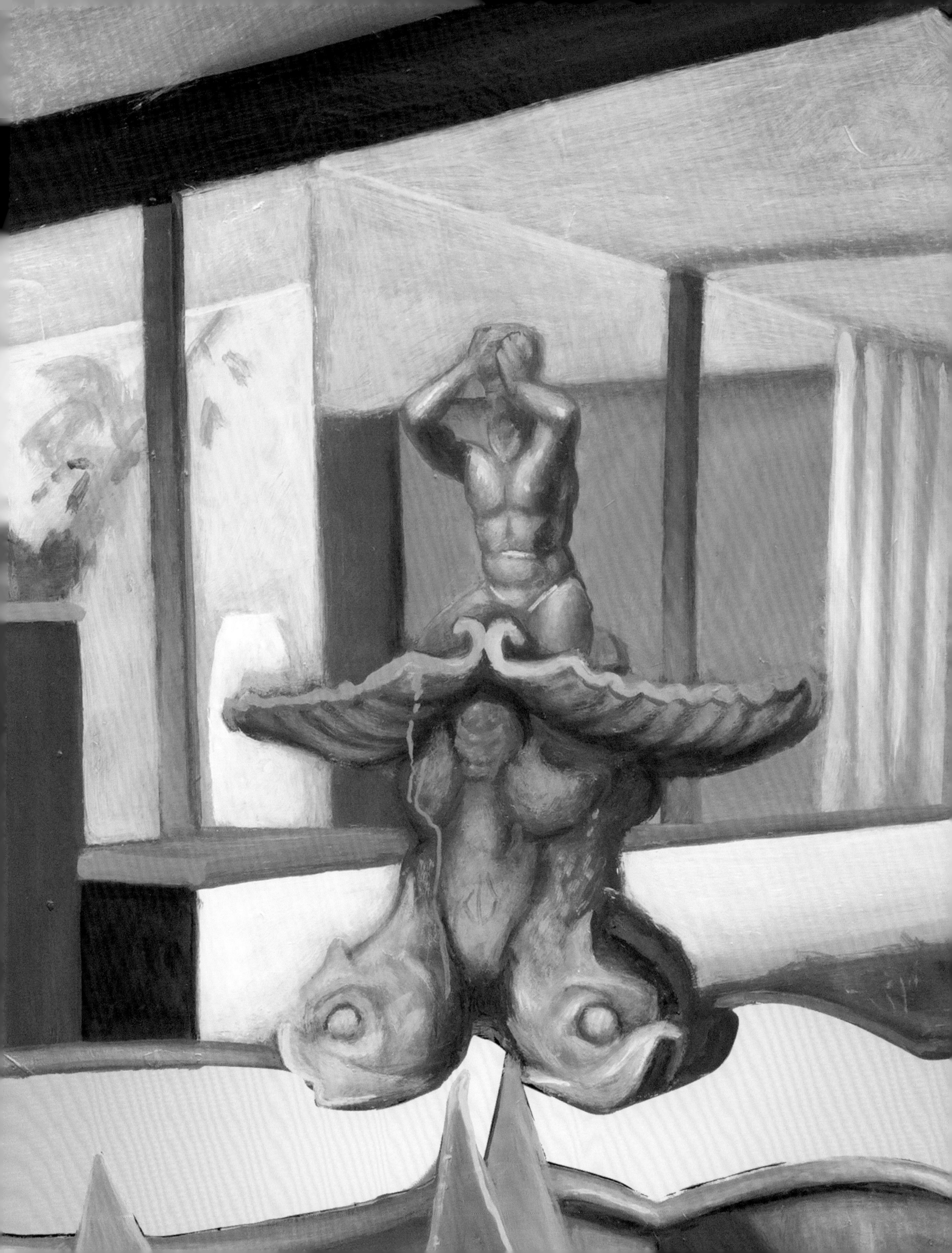

Mulholland Drive

2018
Oil and enamel on mirror
25 × 32 inches (63.5 × 81.3 cm)

Marmont Avenue

2018
Oil and enamel on mirror
25 × 32 inches (63.5 × 81.3 cm)

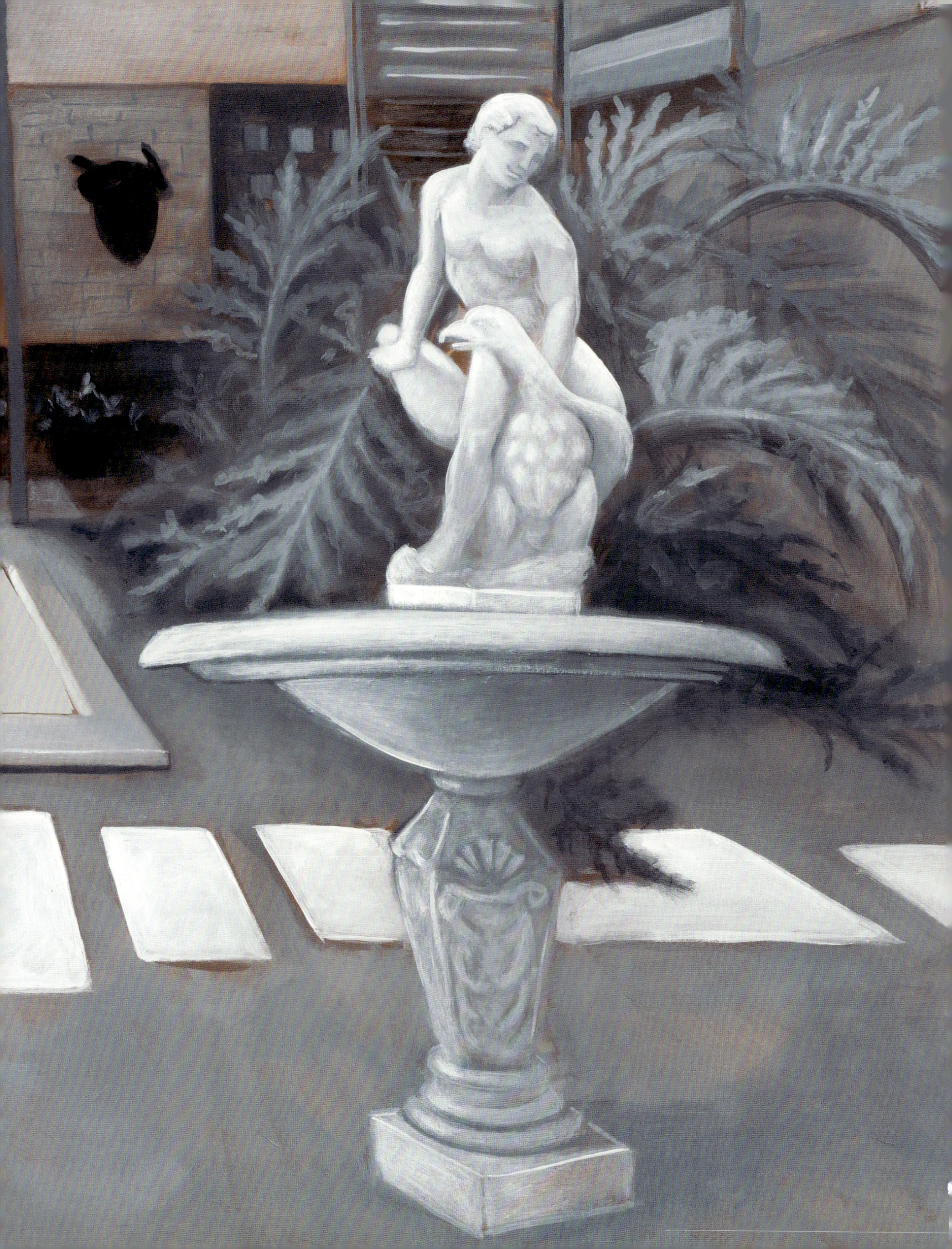

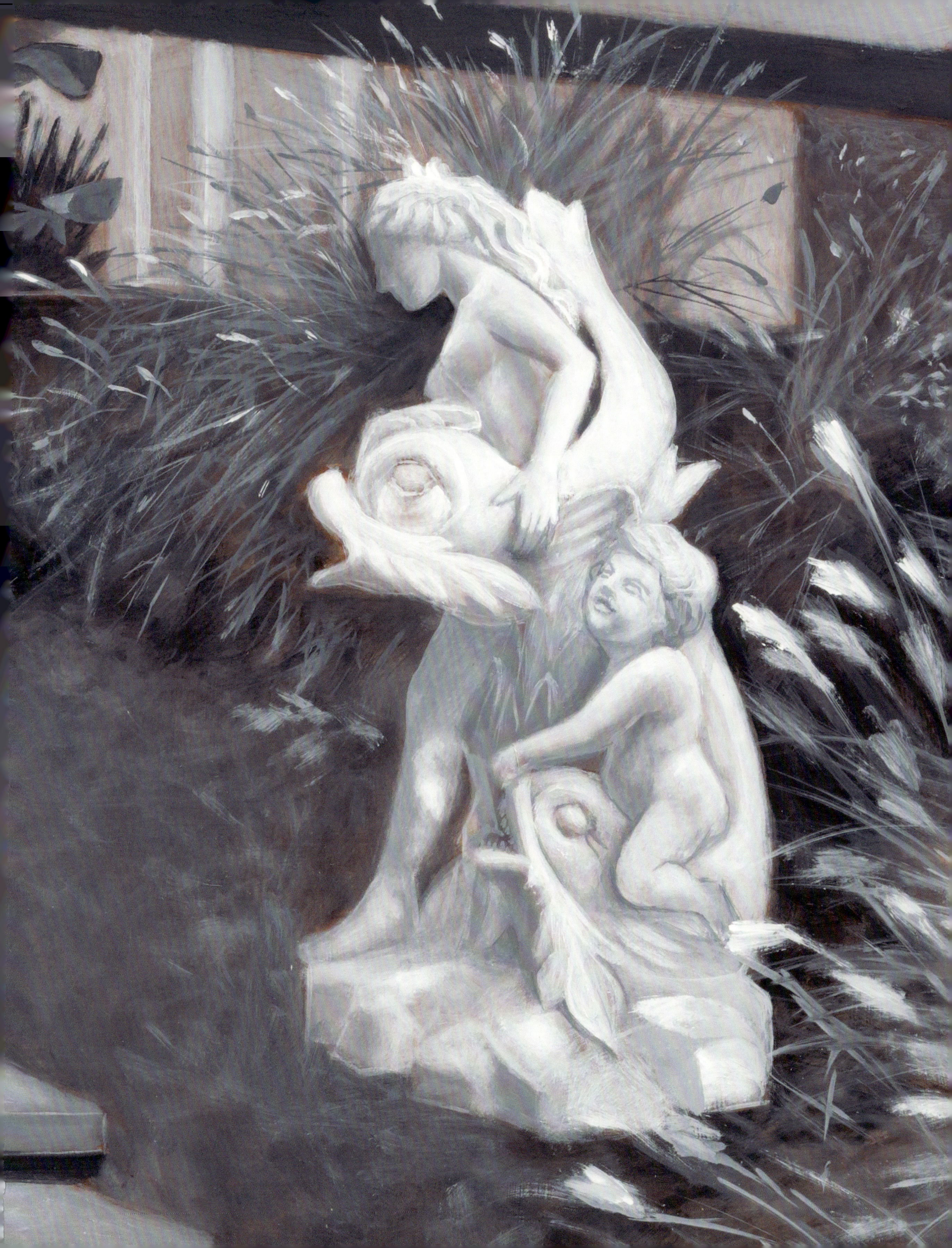

Once upon a Time...

PAMELA GOLBIN

Enriched by cultural and stylistic back-and-forths, Rachel Feinstein's vision includes quotations from sources as diverse as baroque sculpture, rococo art and decor, religious iconography, Second Empire wallpaper, and Art Deco architecture. In her sculpture, drawings, paintings, and installations, this reworked iconography—whose strange ambivalence feels taken from real life and then reconstructed in some unexpected matter—is all blended together and always hits the target.

Like a distorted mirror image of the American dream, Feinstein's oeuvre plays with references to the incredible variety of European history and the beauty of its culture, its high-end refinement, its cult of luxury, and the extreme sophistication of savoir faire passed down through the generations. Her work blends references to the grandeur and prestige of patrons, and to the splendor of the elite, but also conjures the decadence and fall of royal houses and the aristocracy.

Yet a critical, even parodic dimension seems to contaminate her otherwise scholarly investigations, these excavations of history's strata (on both a micro and a macro scale), these layers of successive memories, these recumbent, piled-up traces from which time itself flows and spreads while constantly savoring its own historical ubiquity.

In Feinstein's work, the essential takes place discreetly, anonymously, secretly, and mysteriously, as in the fairy tales she loves so much. If you look carefully—beyond the overflow of information that continues to burst forth and remove the essential focus from sight—everything seems to happen via sleight of hand. With a wave of her magic wand, Sleeping Beauty steals away and Prince Charming really does disappear into thin air, gone without leaving a forwarding address. What remains of these sudden disappearances, more than the trace of a sign, is a classic fairy-tale symbol: Cinderella's glass slipper. In *Corine* and *Octavio* (both 2018), two porcelain sculptures made for the exhibition *Secrets* at Gagosian Beverly Hills, the typical commedia dell'arte characters have vanished, leaving only their shoes delicately posed on top of oversize pedestals, which are like erectile, distorted, anamorphic seashells, tactile settings par excellence. The shoes become the fourfold proof of the figures' presence and their absence, of their passage between two parallel worlds of art.

This presence in no way obscures the emptiness—evanescent, ghostly, evocative—that they have left behind. "Nature abhors a void," said Aristotle, and so with an unavoidable Pavlovian reflex, it is immediately filled to the brim by our imaginations. This shadow at the heart of the work, this seemingly absent subliminal machinery, is the start of a voyage through time and space—a journey through the spiral shell of a dream within a dream, which reveals a cleverly hidden alcove inserted deep inside the mechanism itself. Then, through a secret door to a strong room walled up in silence, a complex machine room, an intimate space of watchmaker-like precision and artistic creativity.

To sum up: In these sculptures, you might say that what is missing is actually the ultimate referent, the power of attraction, the palpable tension of the "thing," another form of an even more physical gravitational pull. Or to employ the terminology of Surrealist filmmaker Luis Buñuel, what is missing is "that obscure object of desire."

The Sacred and the Profane

Feinstein admits to a twofold fascination, a double-edged interest, in both the wealth of European culture and how Americans assimilate it, digest it, remodel it, and then give it new purpose by maximizing its potential. She is interested in how her fellow citizens confidently appropriate European culture without ever really trying to understand its foundations or uncover its inherent values. And she wants to show that the result of this assimilation, its logical conclusion, is the ultimate in flashiness, the absolute embodiment of grandiloquent artifacts, of sometimes unfiltered tackiness in overly made-up Technicolor kitsch—a place where serial copies in turn become new sources of inspiration.

The Domain of All Possibilities

In 2000, Feinstein went on another journey, not through time and space, but to Bavaria. This voyage was far more anchored in the real, even if it remained an allegorical homage. While the common denominator of the sites she visited in southern Germany was their picturesque settings, each one prettier than the last, what Feinstein found most satisfying, more than this sparkling diversity, was encountering the superb Nymphenburg porcelain works in Munich. Seized by a passion while wandering through the factory's magnificent collections of porcelain figures, she felt as though a spell had been cast, with the tacit blessing of the same nymphs—symbols of Mother Nature's creative and productive activities—from whom the works took their name. Enchanted and charmed, Feinstein by her own admission succumbed instantly to an infamous condition that has affected so many collector-aesthetes and enlightened amateurs since the eighteenth century.

"Porcelain Sickness"

According to one French source, collectors can be split into two distinct categories: "cupboard collectors," who amass works of art simply for the pleasure of it, and "window collectors," who prefer to exhibit their finds. Both have fallen under the same spell, however: they suffer from the syndrome known as "acute collectionitis": a compulsion, an irrepressible desire, to accumulate objects of great value, each of which provokes an emotional reaction similar to a swoon.

King of Poland Augustus II the Strong qualified his own longing for this precious and fragile material, not a little playfully and ironically, as "porcelain sickness." It was during his reign, in 1708 to be exact, that alchemist Johann Friedrich Böttger produced the formula for making hard-paste porcelain. The king then founded the Royal Porcelain Manufactory in Meissen, Germany, and watched as its fame and influence spread across the royal courts of Europe, which had become quickly infatuated with this admirable new "white gold."

When Feinstein returned to the United States from Bavaria, her obsession was with Franz Anton Bustelli (1723–1763), the most celebrated porcelain modeler of his time.

She began to work on a series of majolica sculptures based on his renowned porcelain figurines depicting characters from the commedia dell'arte, an improvised form of theater originating in Italy and popular throughout Europe during the sixteenth through eighteenth centuries. Feinstein's sculptures *Octavio* and *Corine* retained only the rocaille supporting structures of Bustelli's originals, withdrawing the eponymous characters and replacing them solely with their shoes, varnished and adorned with square golden buckles. Contrary to appearances, the story of Octavio and Corine is neither innocent nor anodyne, and their disappearance is even less so. Octavio and Corine are part of a group of stock characters called *gli innamorati* ("the lovers," in Italian), around whom the drama revolves, and whose roles are more self-consciously elegant and refined than truculent or comic. Unlike other members of a commedia dell'arte troupe, the actors playing *gli inamorati* wear no masks. So it is adieu to the puppy-dog eyes of the characters in the original figurines and the amorous tension of physically separated partners. Yet even after they have taken their leave, there remains the privilege of catching a fleeting, admiring glimpse of their absence, their new incarnation, like the oyster that only delivers its rare and precious pearl once it has been relieved of its protective shell.

No thing, no self, no form, no principle, is safe,
everything is undergoing an invisible but ceaseless transformation.
—Robert Musil[1]

While initially conceptualizing the Bustelli-inspired statues at her studio in Maine, Feinstein suddenly understood that she could only resolve her problems with them by going straight to the source. Instead of using high-density foam or other materials with which she had worked in the past, why not have life-size versions made in porcelain, in situ, in Munich, in the still-functioning Nymphenburg ateliers? Why not create a link between the ancients and the moderns? Classicism and the high-tech would come together, joined hand in hand in anticipation of their model complementarity.

Les Très Riches Heures

Faithful to her system of creating multiple layers of references and collages of borrowings, Feinstein began a series of paintings directly on the smooth surfaces of mirrors. Their points of departure (and anchorage) were the wallpapers *Rêve de bonheur* and *Les plaisirs champêtres*, the former created by French manufactory Jules Desfossé in 1852, the latter by Louis de Carmontelle in 1785. Study these slices of life expatriated from their usual frames of reference and placed into another context, and Feinstein's illusion is perfect. The eighteenth and nineteenth centuries easily and naturally slip into their new milieus; there is no concertinaing or kaleidoscoping. These figures fit right in next to these modern houses and vehicles, as if both have always been there together. Looked at this way, the mirrored backgrounds assume dual roles of medium and disrupter, like spanners in the well-oiled works. These untouched spaces, unpainted fragments that are cleverly and logically integrated into the painting, also catch and reflect the passing viewer's eyes. They create an original, intrusive sense of narration, performing a constant interaction between the spectator's fleeting, eruptive gaze and the work's fluid flatness. In short, they create diffracted mise en abymes into which we can project ourselves.

The Mirror and Its Reflective Power

Object of all number of fantasies and illusions, the mirror—magic or not—cannot lie because it symbolizes the whole truth and nothing but the truth, even when that truth is of the kind that would be better left unsaid. Or, as the Brothers Grimm put it:

> *"Mirror, mirror, on the wall,*
> *Who in this land is fairest of all?"*
> *It answered:*
> *"You, my queen, are fair; it is true.*
> *But Snow White is a thousand times fairer than you."*[2]

From Lewis Carroll to Jean Cocteau, reflective surfaces have also been made to be passed through. Yet today, the global trend is toward reflective surfaces of photographic narcissism. Indeed, the slightest glance caught in our new selfie mirrors now seems able to summon all the electrifying energy of Versailles's Hall of Mirrors, as if the Sun King himself were being reflected and illuminating the world with his light. Feinstein's use of the mirror, however, is more distanced, playful, and provocative. Her desire is to embrace the viewer's gaze, to include and involve each person in this intimate confrontation, even temporarily, as though giving the ultimate nod to all the parameters she has put into place.

A Small Treatise on Contemporary Alchemy

What if the Old World disappeared completely, leaving only the New? What if it underwent a metamorphosis, turning into Little Red Riding Hood under the guidance of Bluebeard, the ogre who owns seven-league boots, and Ali Baba and his cavern? Like an out-of-control, wildly spinning fairy tale caught on reality TV. From then on, we would be able to jump into the disenchanted story of the wicked fairy godmother going shopping in the local mall, duplicated across the world by infinite selfies. And as if by magic, it would be set on endless repeat, virtually inscribed for eternity.

Time Regained

In Feinstein's shape-shifting oeuvre, there is not calm, but rather an Olympian chaos created by a masterful hand in direct contact with the rhythm of modern life. Her work is a perfectly measured patchwork of the now, an antechamber of a vast investigative field ready to be explored, again and again, always. It is like the heterotopia that theoreticians paint as the physical geolocalization of utopia: concrete, tangible spaces that play host to the imaginary, like a child's cabin perched high up in the trees or trompe l'oeil scenery in a theater. Above all, like Feinstein, the heterotopia juxtaposes different spaces that are clearly incompatible in the real world in one single place.

Feinstein's work is an open-air oeuvre, inhabited from the inside, a landscape with signage that is bewildering because it anticipates the timeless. Her work also passes on the baton of the avant-garde, beautifully creating its own position in the genetic heritage of yesterday, today, and tomorrow.

1. Robert Musil, *The Man Without Qualities, Vol. 1*, trans. Sophie Wilkins and Burton Pike (New York: Vintage, 1996), p. 269.
2. Jacob and Wilhelm Grimm, *Kinder und hausmärchen: gesammelt durch die Brüder Grimm* (Göttingen, Germany: Verlag der Dieterichichen Buchhandlung, 1857), p. 265. Translated by D. L. Ashliman.

List of Works

Bradbury, 2018
Oil and enamel on mirror
42 × 54 inches
(106.7 × 137.2 cm)
pp. 26–27

Corine, 2018
Majolica
51 ¼ × 37 ⅜ × 49 ¼ inches
(130.2 × 95 × 125 cm)
4 unique versions
pp. 12–13

Granite Bay, 2018
Inkjet print and UV semigloss liquid laminate
on wallpaper
Dimensions variable
Edition of 5 + 2 AP
pp. 4–5

The Lake House, 2018
Oil and enamel on mirror
42 × 54 inches
(106.7 × 137.2 cm)
pp. 20–21

Marmont Avenue, 2018
Oil and enamel on mirror
25 × 32 inches
(63.5 × 81.3 cm)
p. 47

Mulholland Drive, 2018
Oil and enamel on mirror
25 × 32 inches
(63.5 × 81.3 cm)
p. 46

Neutra Place, 2018
Oil and enamel on mirror
25 × 32 inches
(63.5 × 81.3 cm)
p. 43

Octavio, 2018
Majolica
39 ½ × 53 ½ × 43 ⅜ inches
(100.3 × 135.9 × 110.2 cm)
4 unique versions
pp. 36–37

Rêve de Bonheur, 2018
Oil and enamel on mirror
42 × 54 inches
(106.7 × 137.2 cm)
pp. 8–9

Scènes de Jardins, 2018
Oil and enamel on mirror
48 × 106 inches
(121.9 × 269.2 cm)
pp. 30–31

Shadow Mountain Drive, 2018
Oil and enamel on mirror
42 × 54 inches
(106.7 × 137.2 cm)
pp. 18–19

Silver Lake Blvd., 2018
Oil and enamel on mirror
25 × 32 inches
(63.5 × 81.3 cm)
p. 42

Sunset Blvd., 2018
Oil and enamel on mirror
42 × 54 inches
(106.7 × 137.2 cm)
pp. 28–29

Published on the occasion of the exhibition

Rachel Feinstein
Secrets

January 11–February 17, 2018

Gagosian Beverly Hills
456 North Camden Drive
Beverly Hills, CA 90210
+1 310 271 9400
www.gagosian.com

Publication © 2019 Gagosian

All artwork © Rachel Feinstein

"Once upon a Time…" © Pamela Golbin
Translated from French by Tom Ridgway

Director: Rebecca Sternthal
Gagosian exhibition coordinators: Madeline Amos, Dean Anes, Ronnie Gunter, Jacqueline Hulburd,
Hannah Kauffman, Melissa Lazarov, Deborah M. McLeod, Courtney Raterman,
Amanda Stoffel, and Sarah Womble

Director of Publications: Alison McDonald
Editor: Priya Bhatnagar
Publication coordinator: David Arkin
Copy editor: Polly Watson

Design by Goto Design, New York
Color separations by Artproduct, Los Angeles
Printed by Pureprint Group, Uckfield, England

All photographs by Jeff McLane, with the exception of the following: pp. 57, 59, and endpapers: Rob McKeever.

All rights reserved. No part of this publication may be reprinted or reproduced in any form or by any electronic,
mechanical, or other means, now known or hereafter invented, including photocopying and recording,
or in any information retrieval system, without prior written permission from the copyright holders.

ISBN 978-1-938748-71-4

Artist's acknowledgments:

Rachel Feinstein would like to thank the
following individuals for their contributions
to this exhibition and book:

Pamela Golbin, for her beautiful essay

Takaya Goto and Lesley Chi
for their thoughtful book design

The painters: John Currin, Richard Phillips,
Sean Landers, Matvey Levenstein, Cecily Brown,
Krista-Louise Smith, Elliot Purse, Yunsung Jang,
and Anna Wakitsch

The Nymphenburg team: Ingrid Harding, Anders Thomas,
Yurika Petroni-Benotto, Janina Berger, Toni Hörl, Sophie
Kölling, Miguel Lockett, Max Loibl, and Eric Maget

Louis Yoh and Sam Kirby Yoh
for alcohol/music/support

Lisa Yuskavage and Sarah Sze
for studio visits and inspiration

Rebecca Sternthal, Deborah M. McLeod, Dean Anes,
Amanda Stoffel, Jacque Hulburd,
Alison McDonald, and Priya Bhatnagar
at Gagosian for everything!

Larry Gagosian, Chrissie Erpf, and Melissa Lazarov
for the love and support
they have always shown me

John, Francis, Hollis, and Flora Currin
for all their love

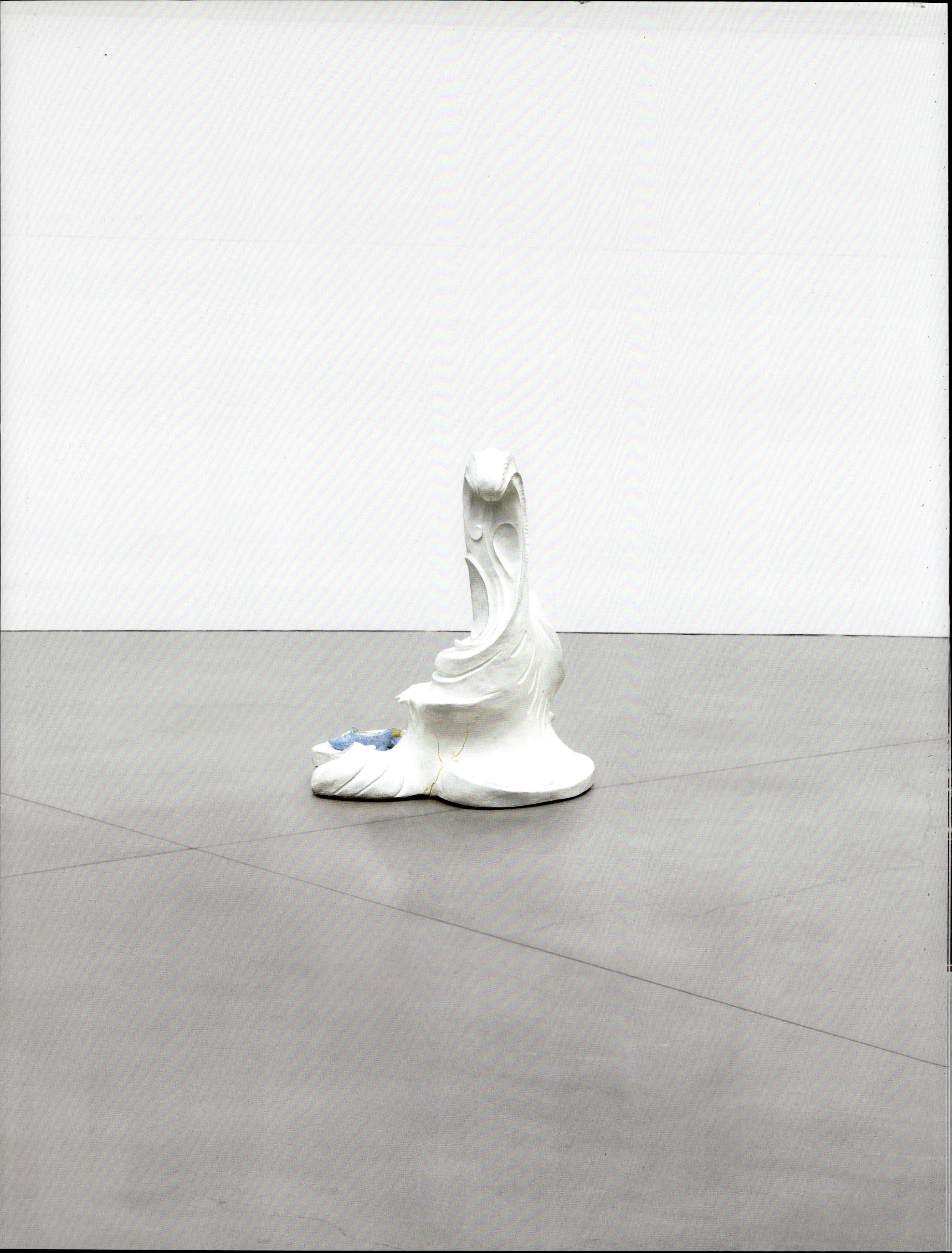

victoria's secret fireworks
BALLERINA ~ LEFT
Fig. 29. The Ottobeuren Master, St Christopher, about 1520. Kunstmuseum, Düsseldorf (Inv. 1936).
BASE
SPATS

Rachel Feinstein

Secrets

Dear Carrie — You are a great Mother + honestly that is harder than being an artist. Trust me. Love, Rachel Feinstein

Jacque is AN AMAZING young WOMAN

GAGOSIAN
Beverly Hills

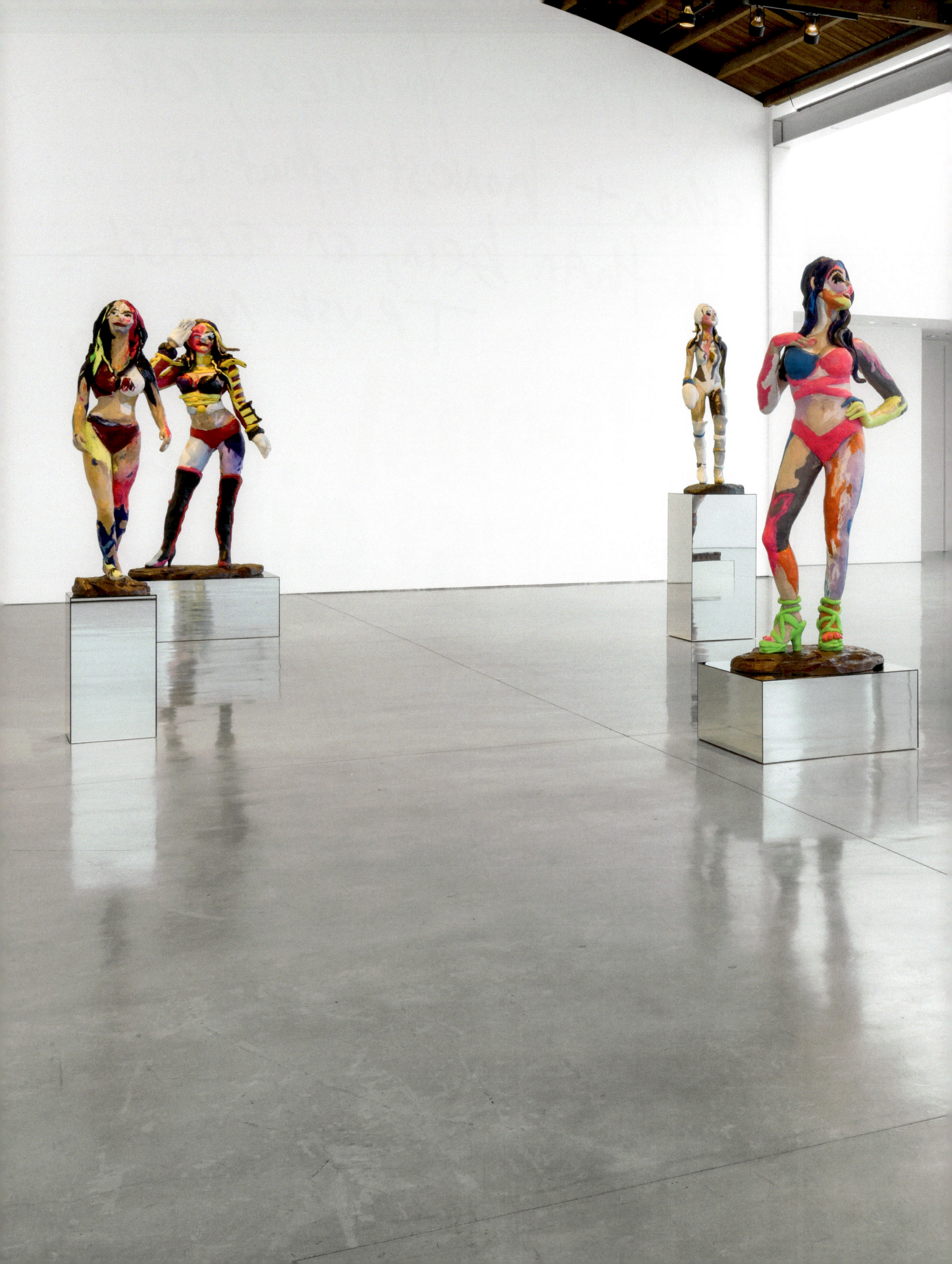

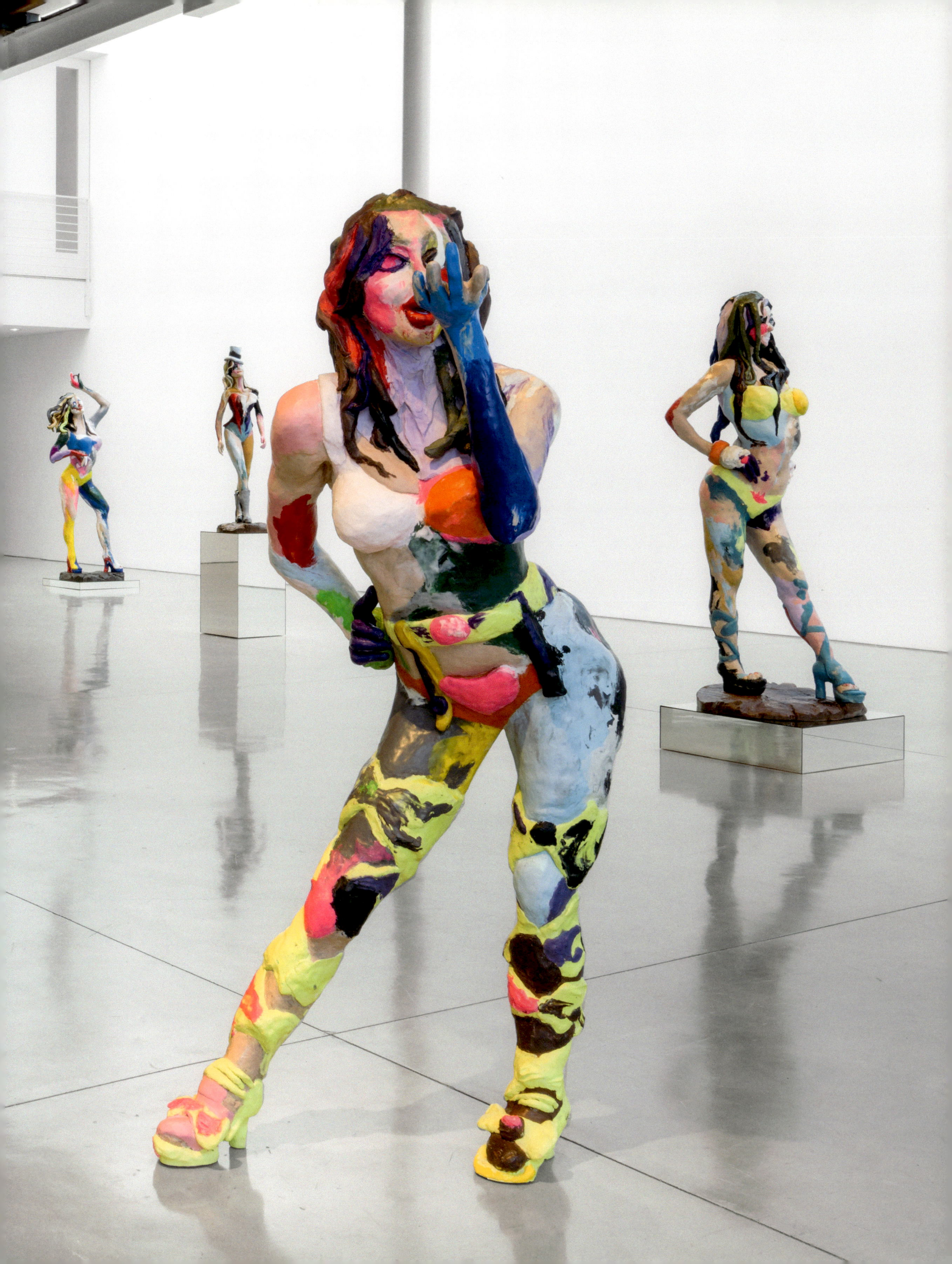

Butterfly

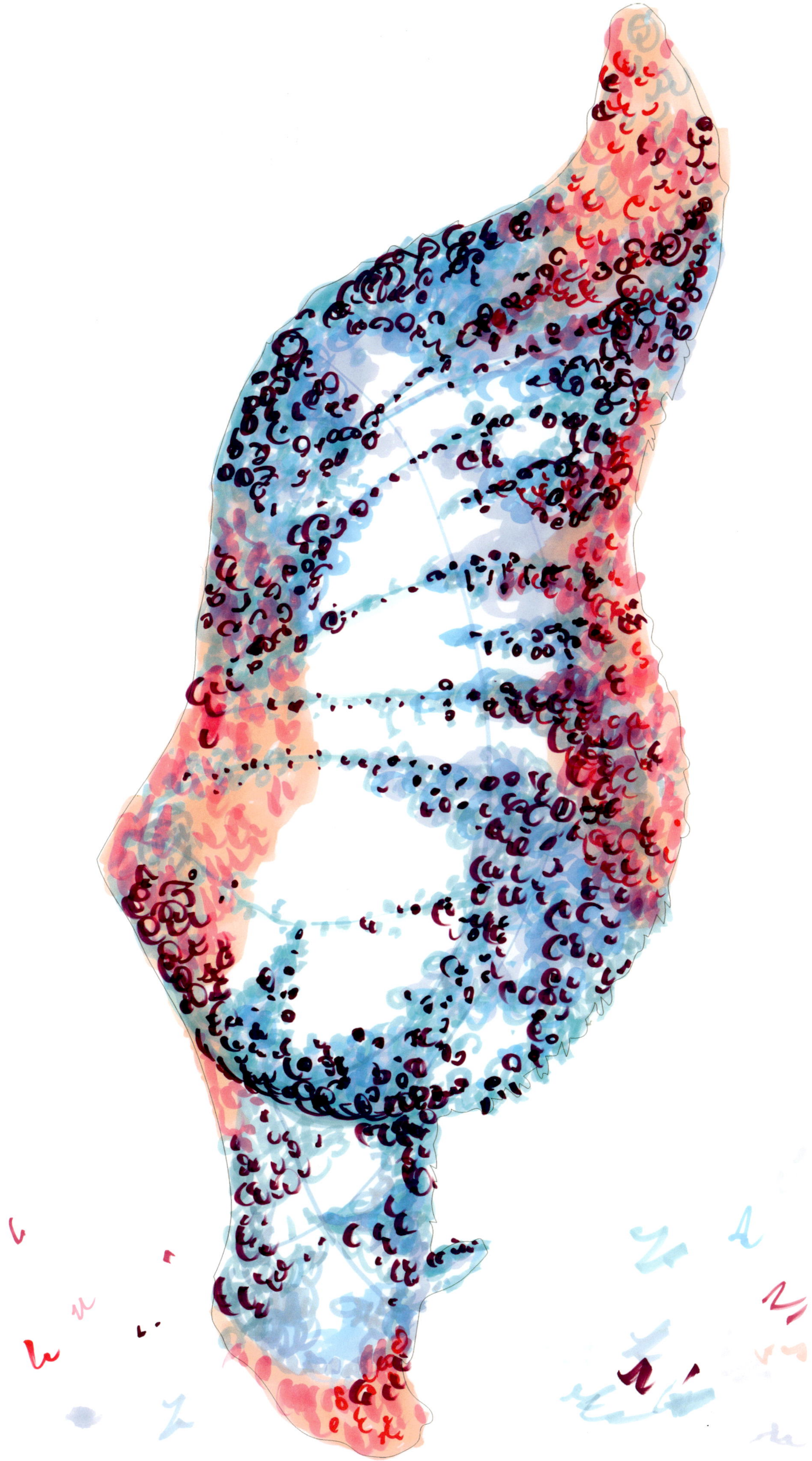

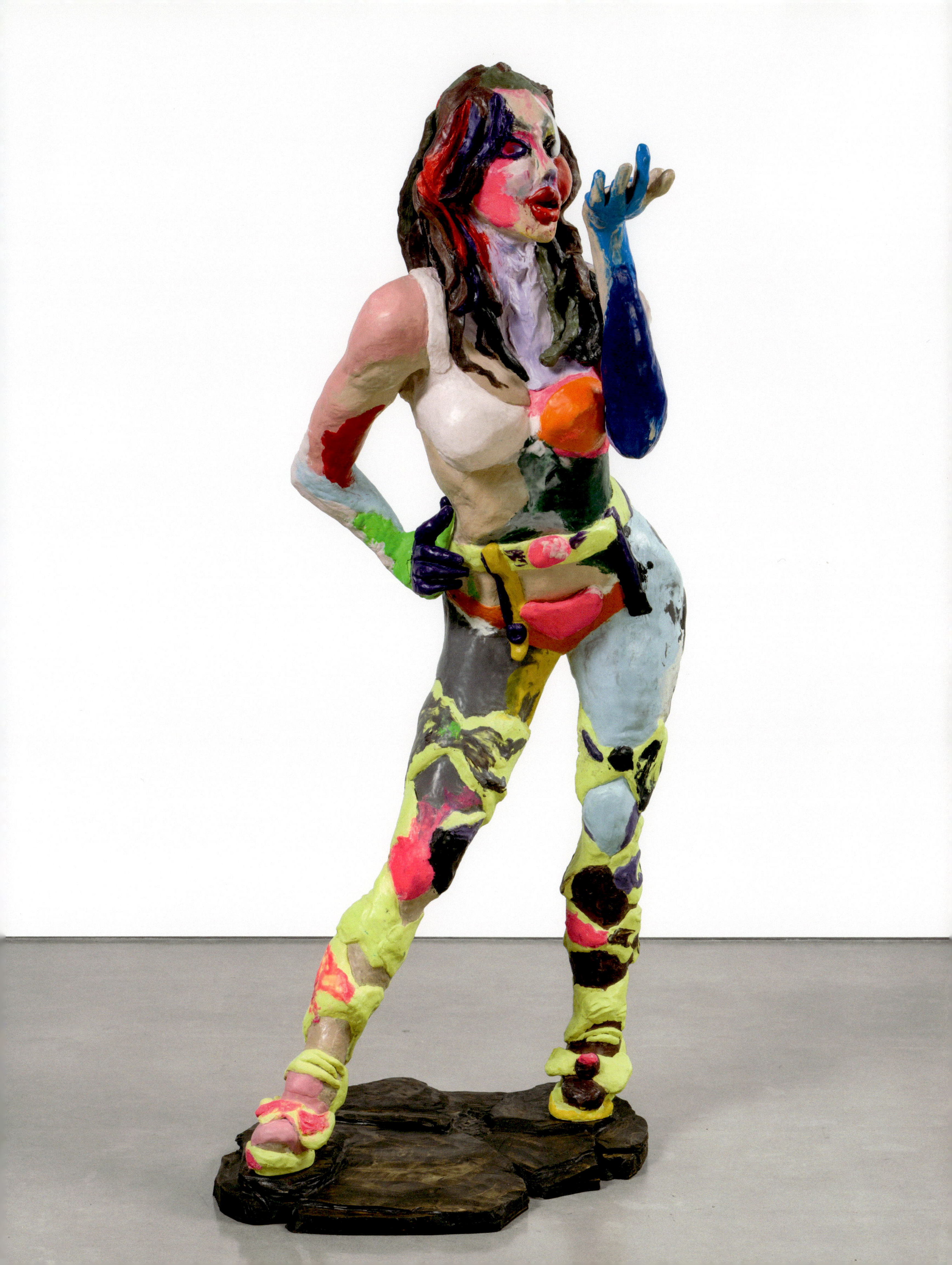

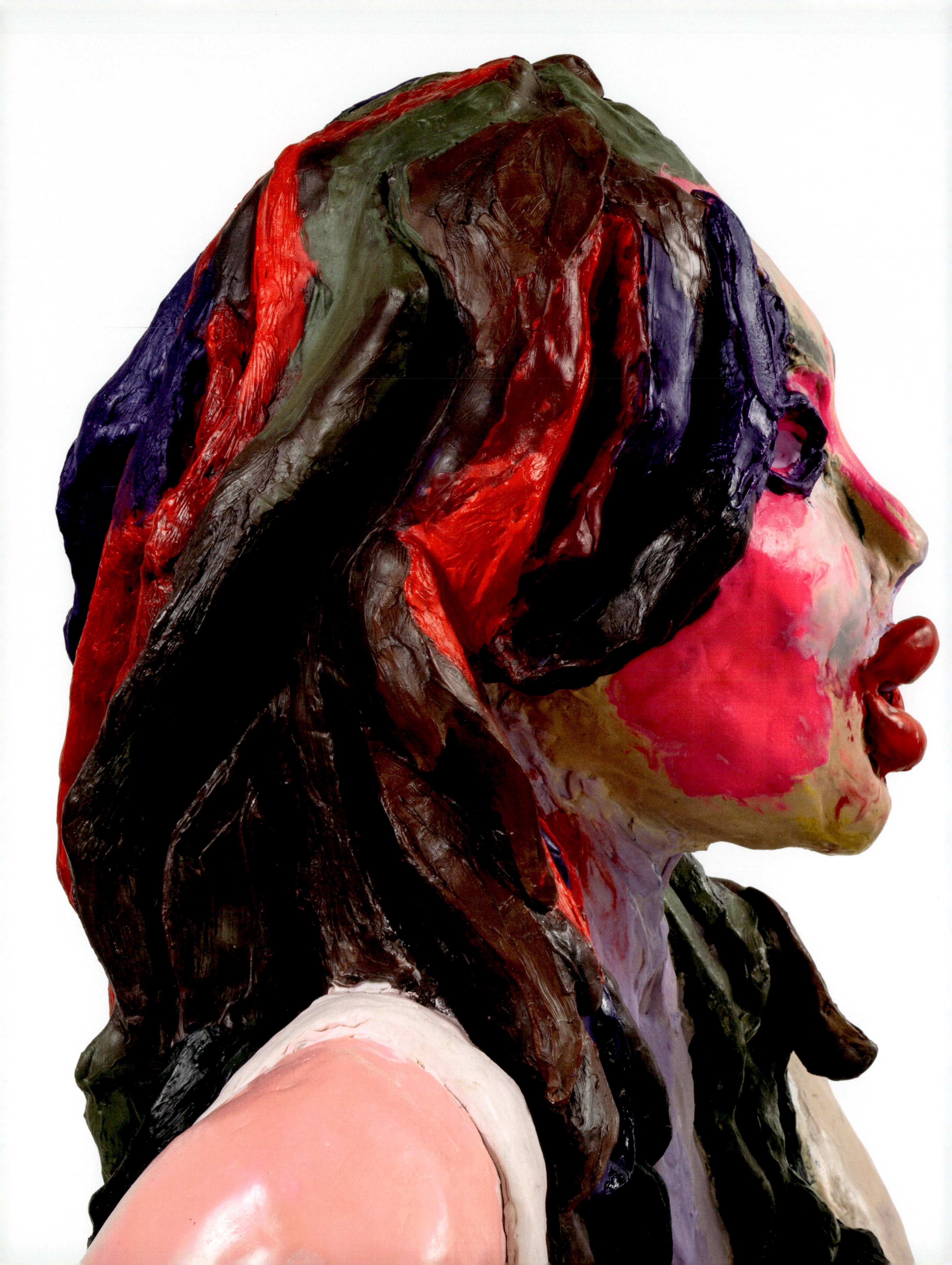

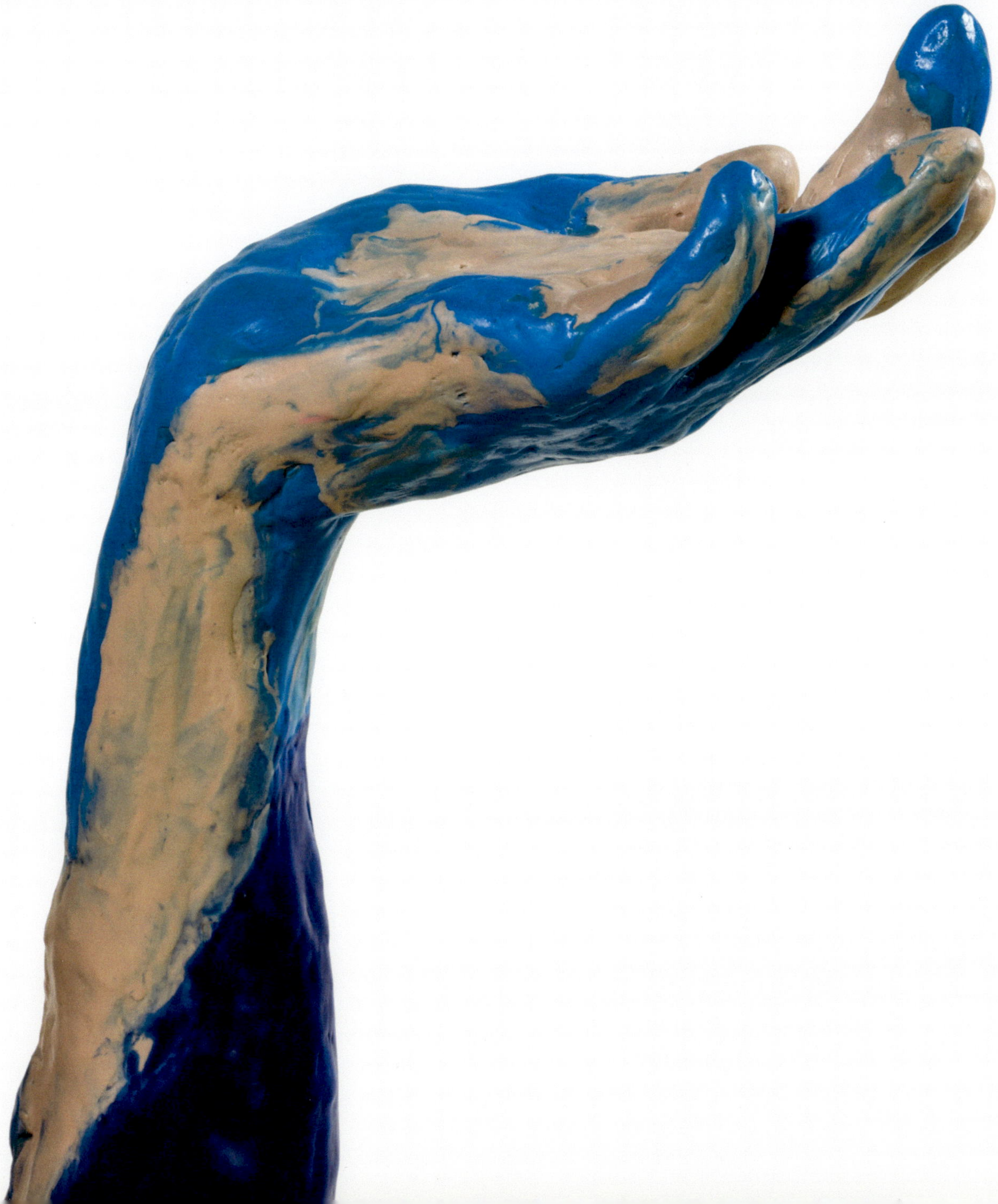

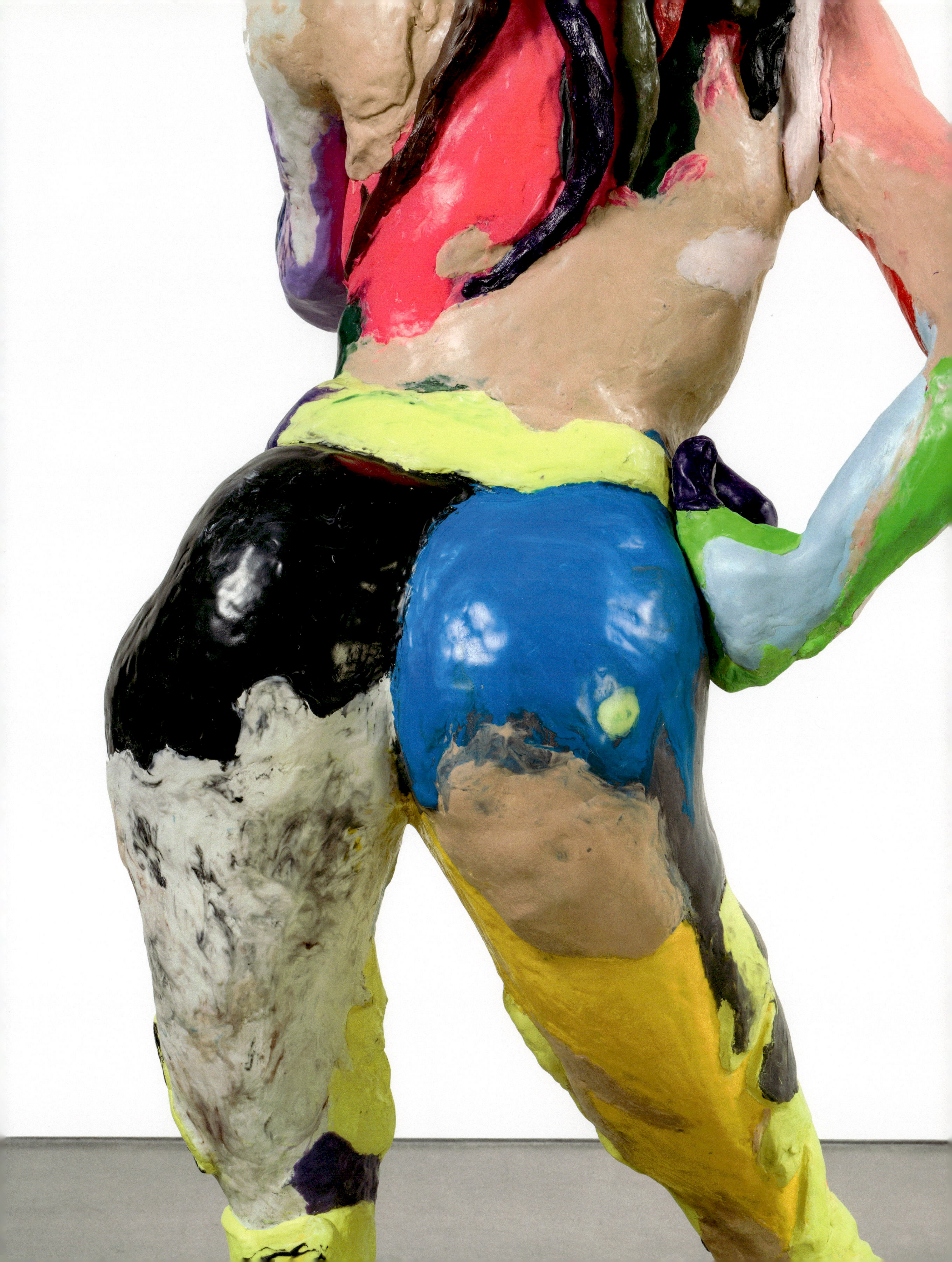

Feathers

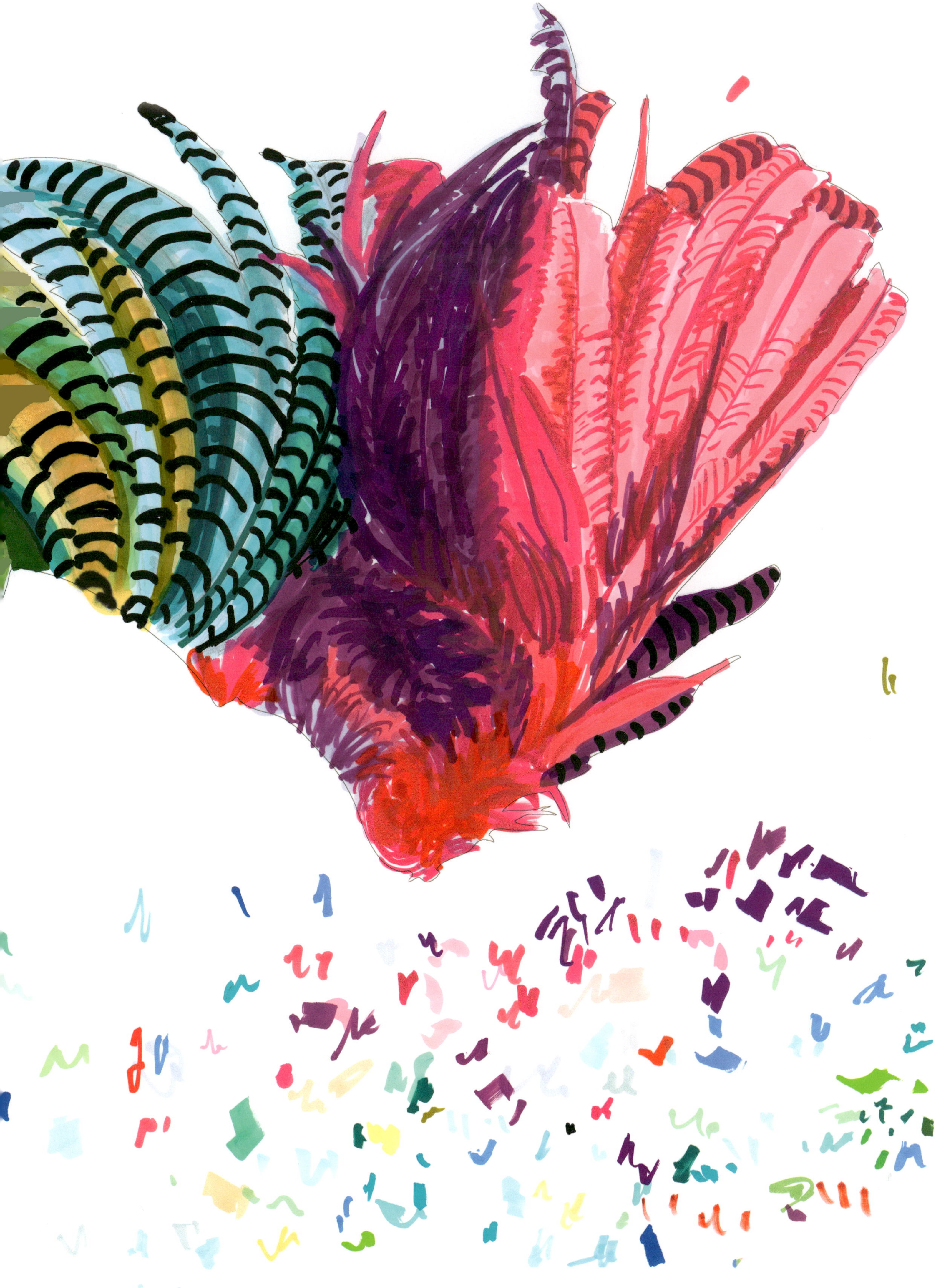

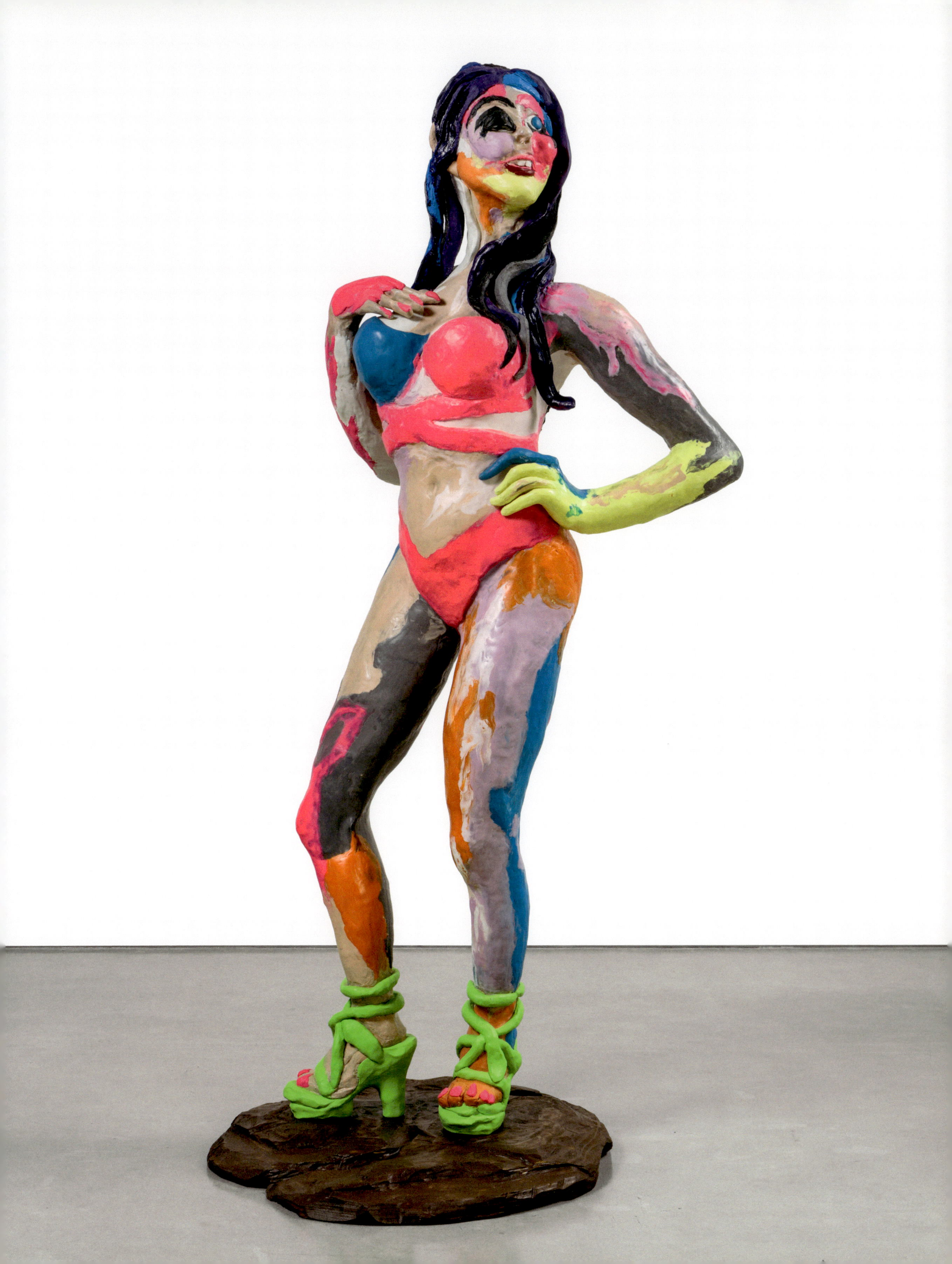

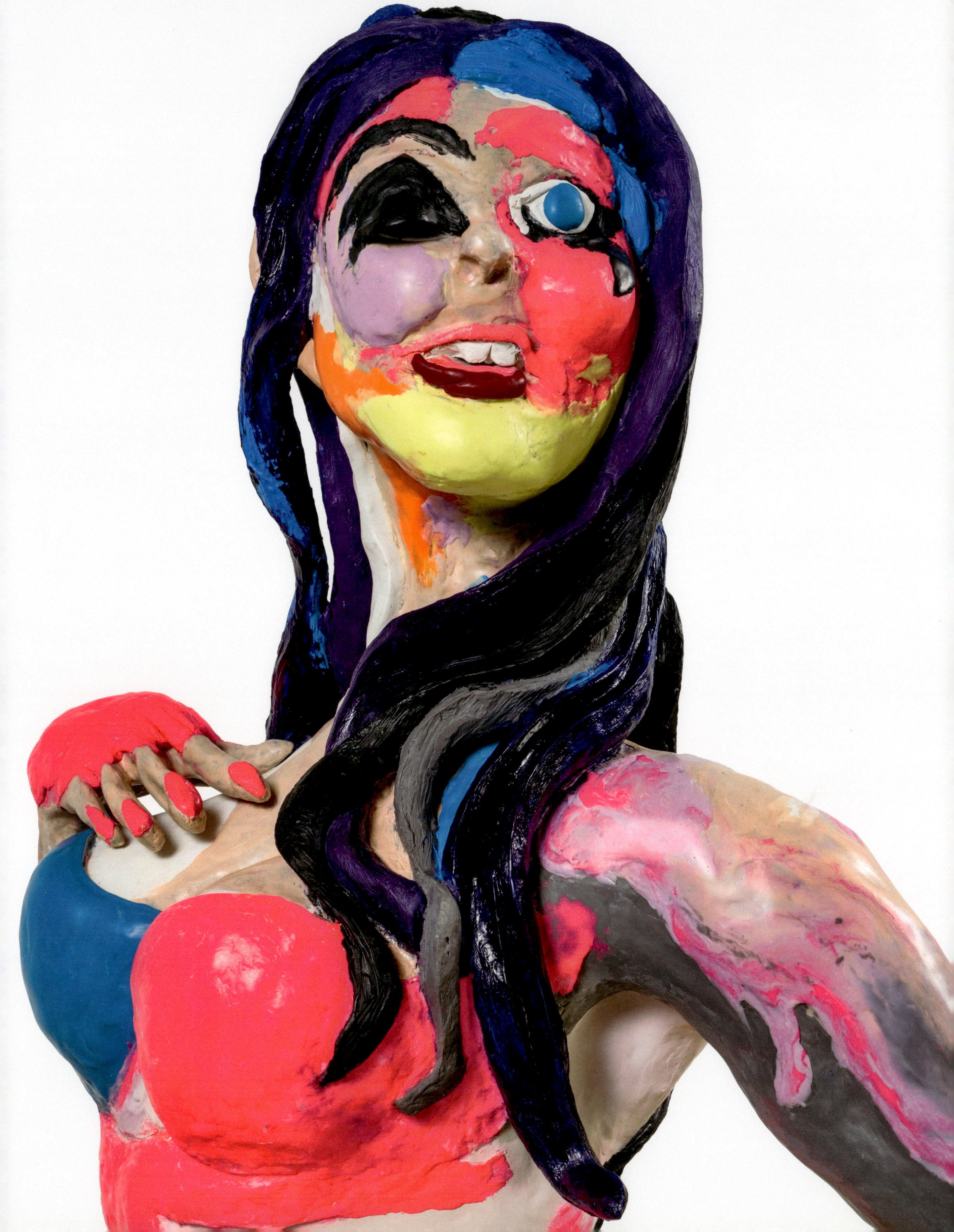

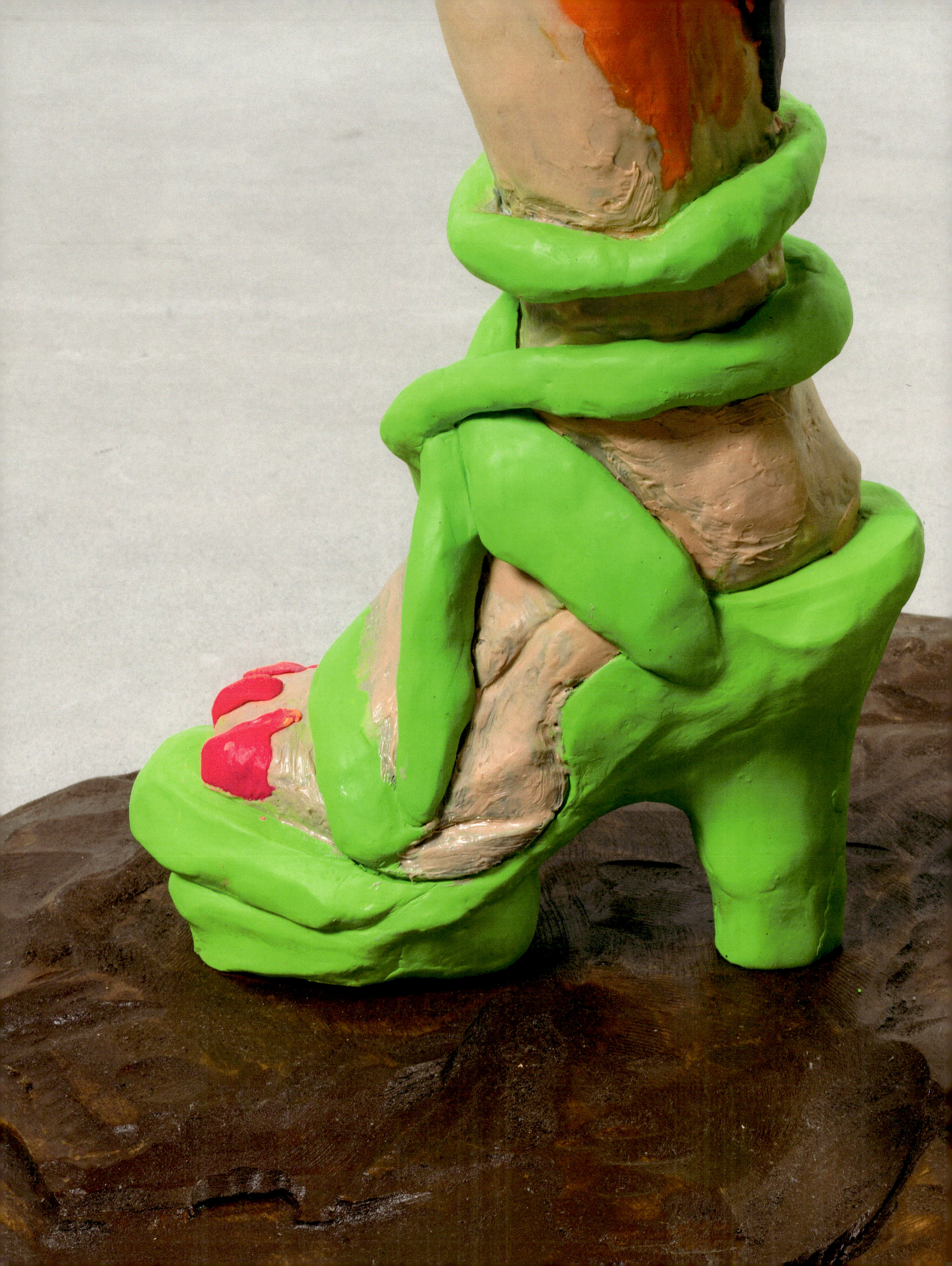

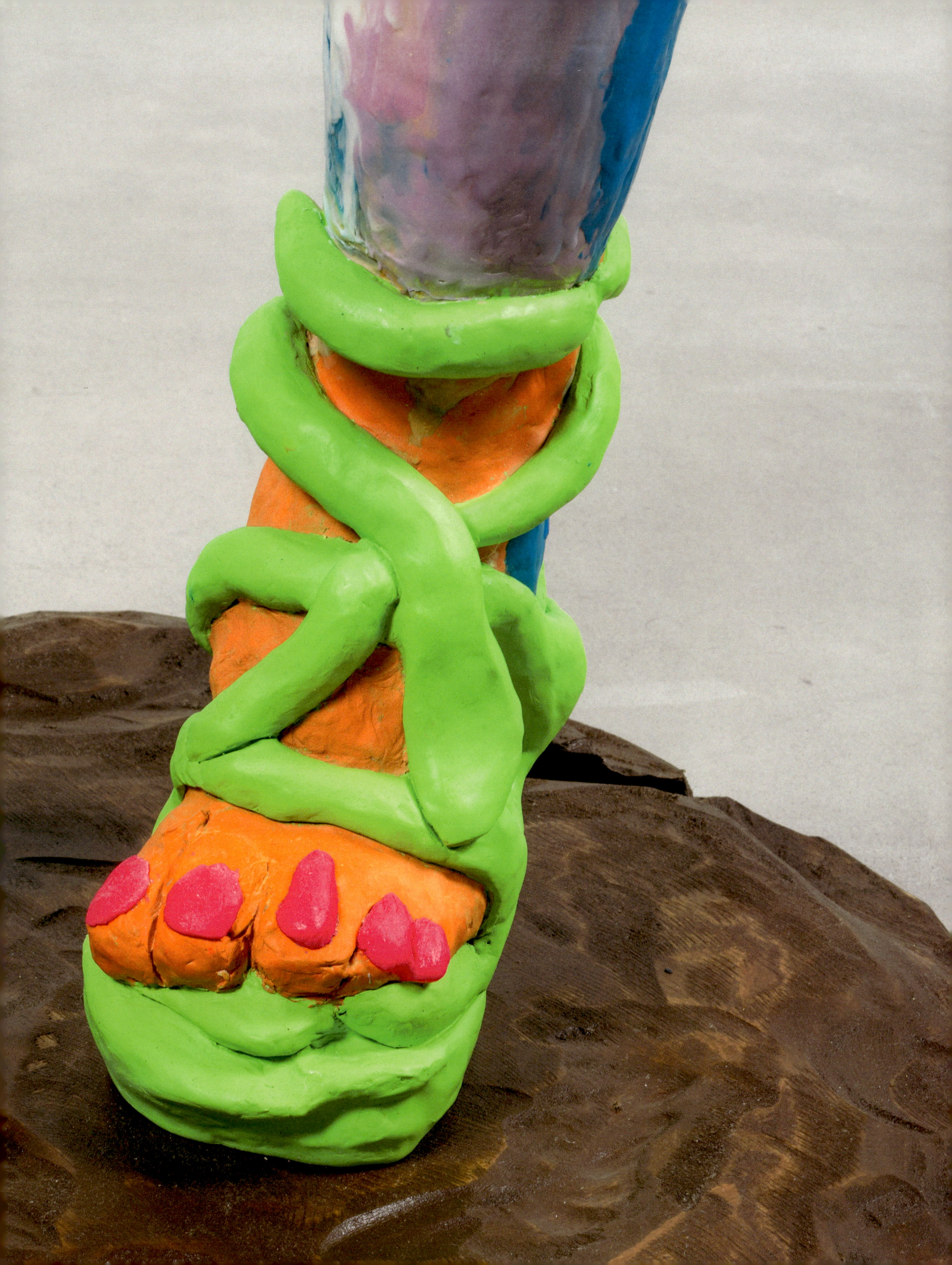

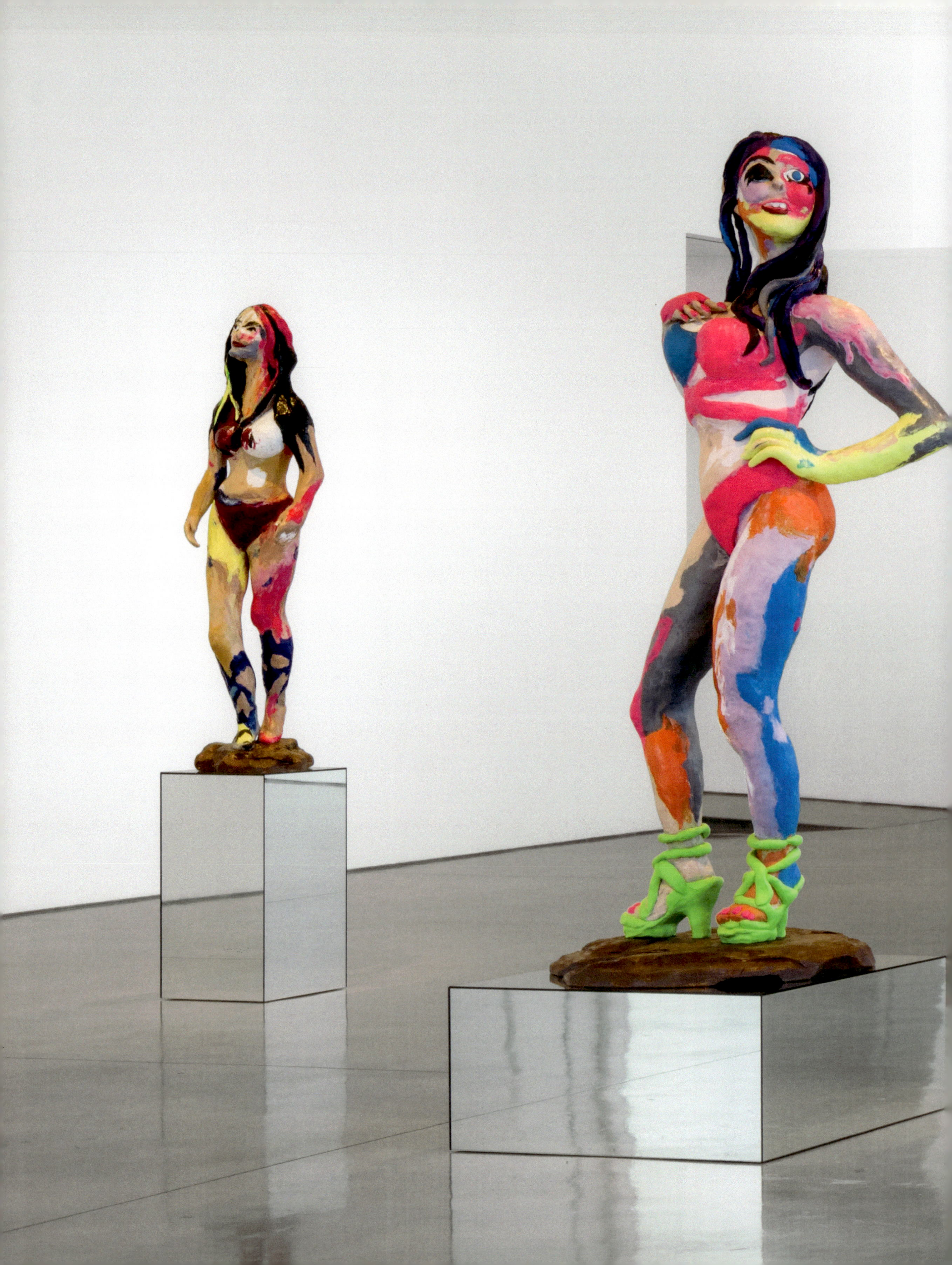

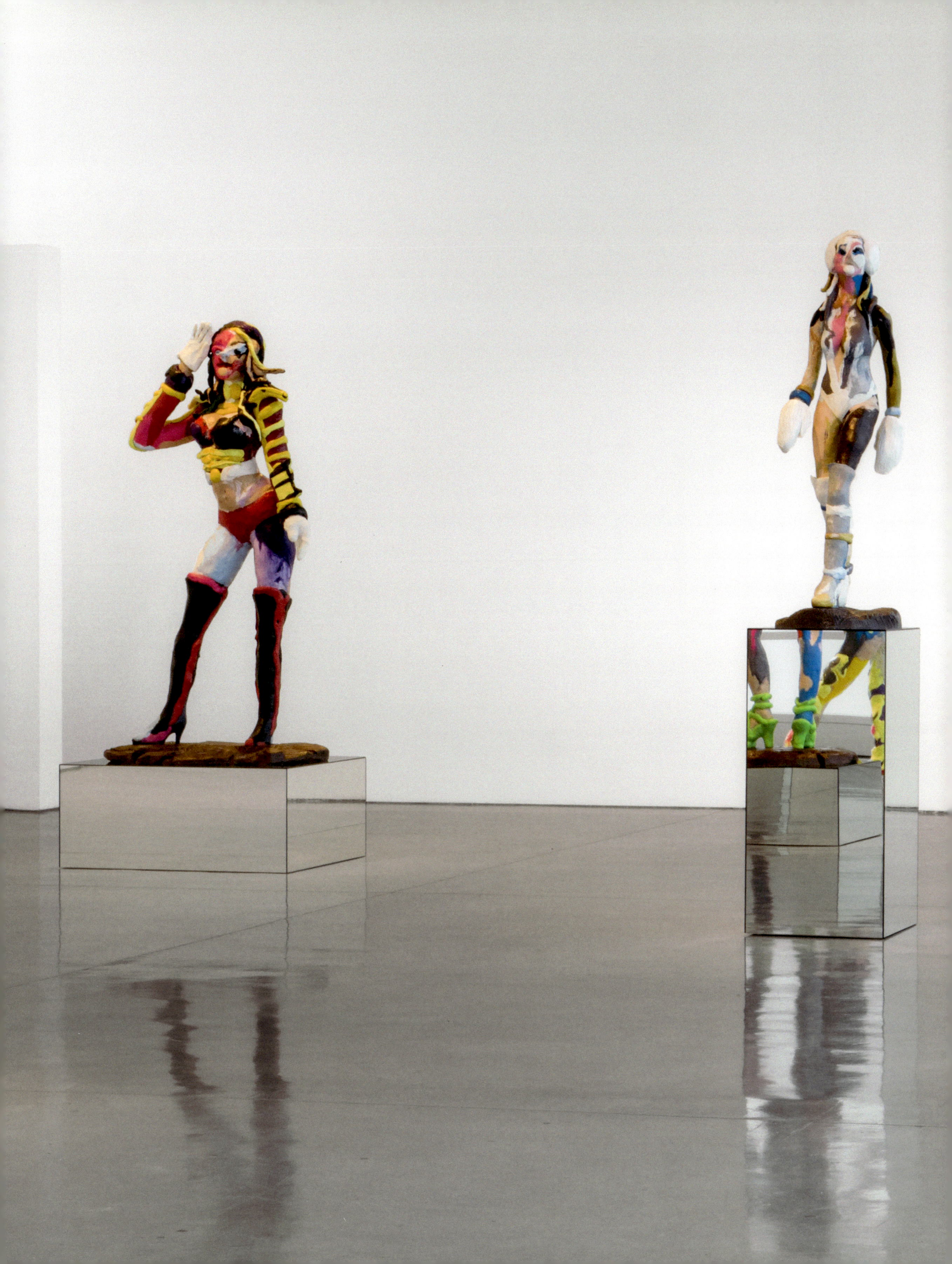

Tourist

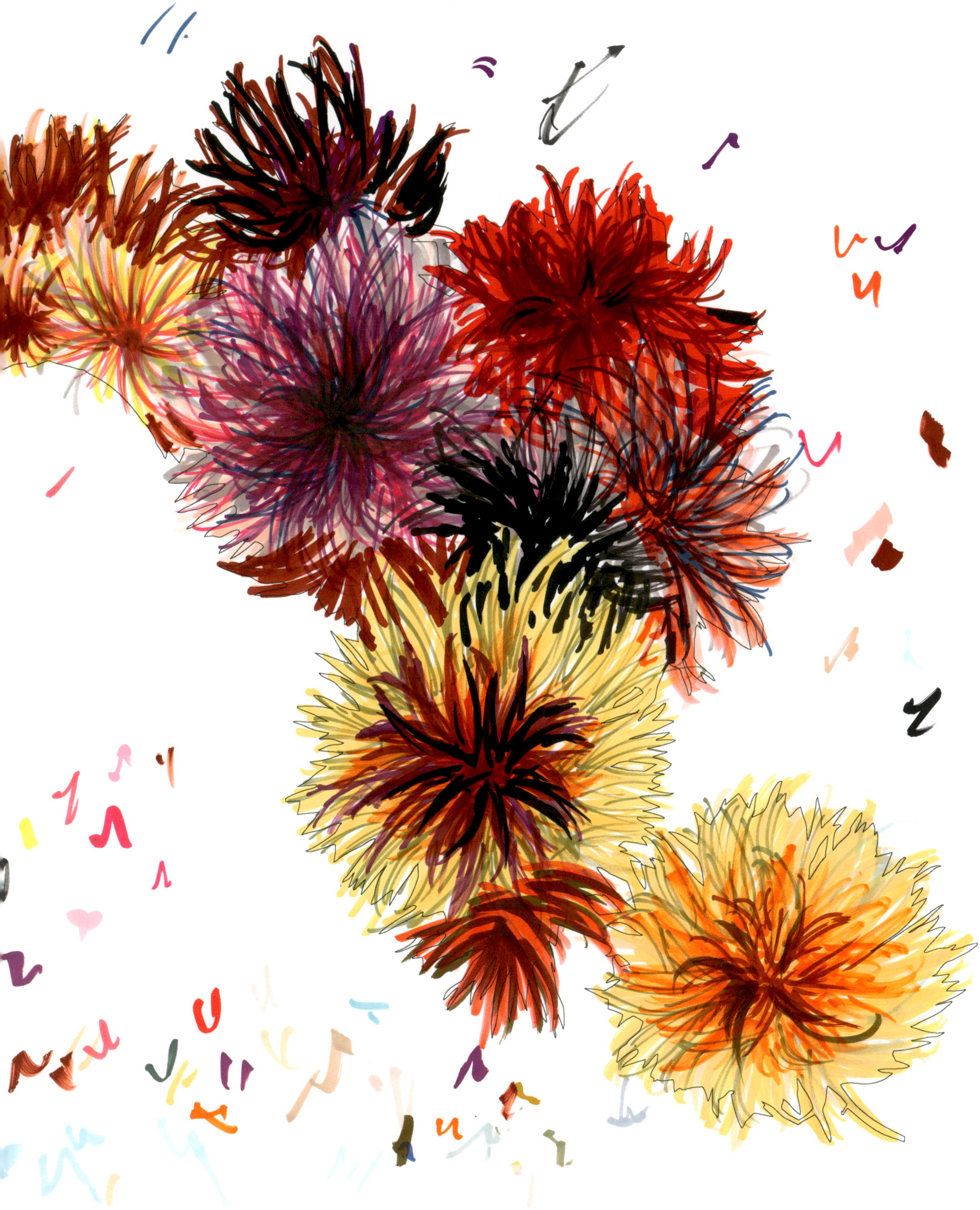

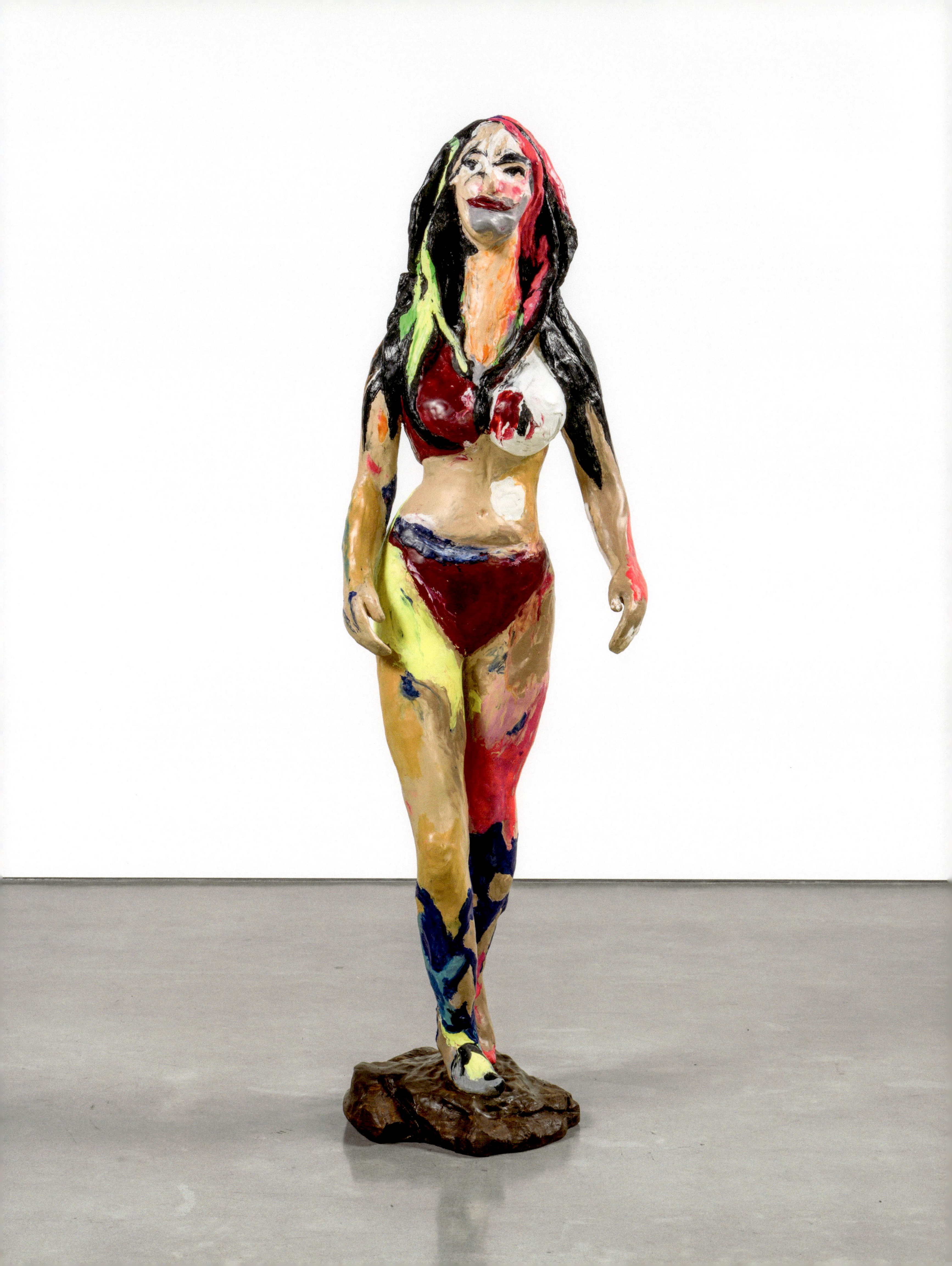

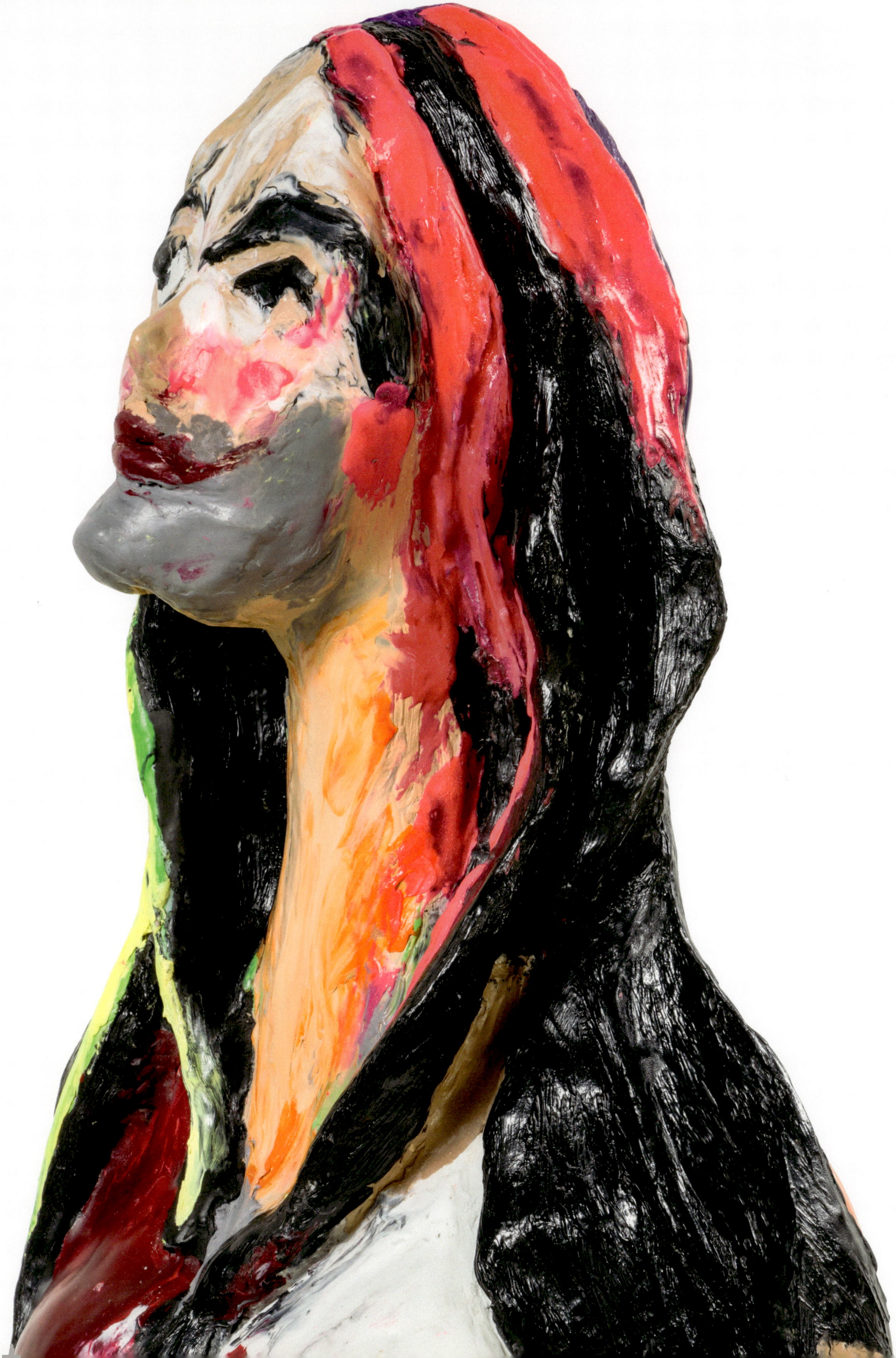

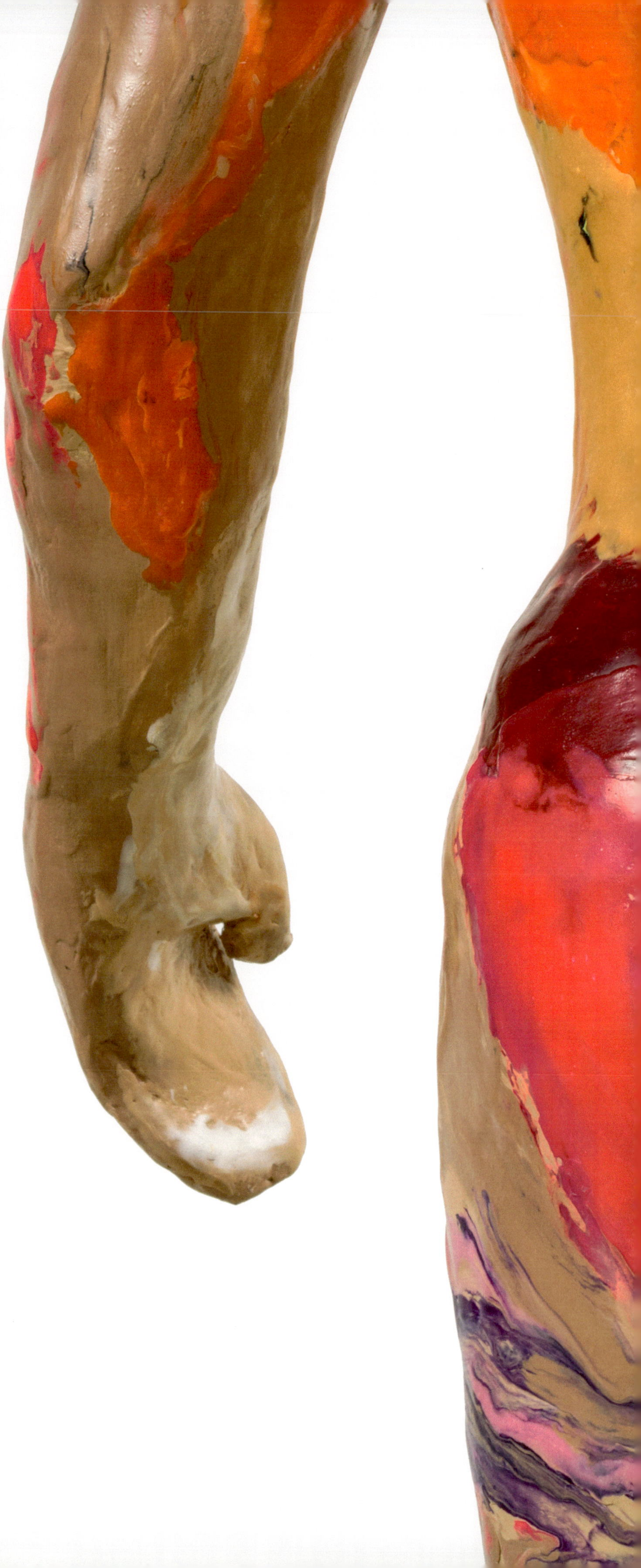

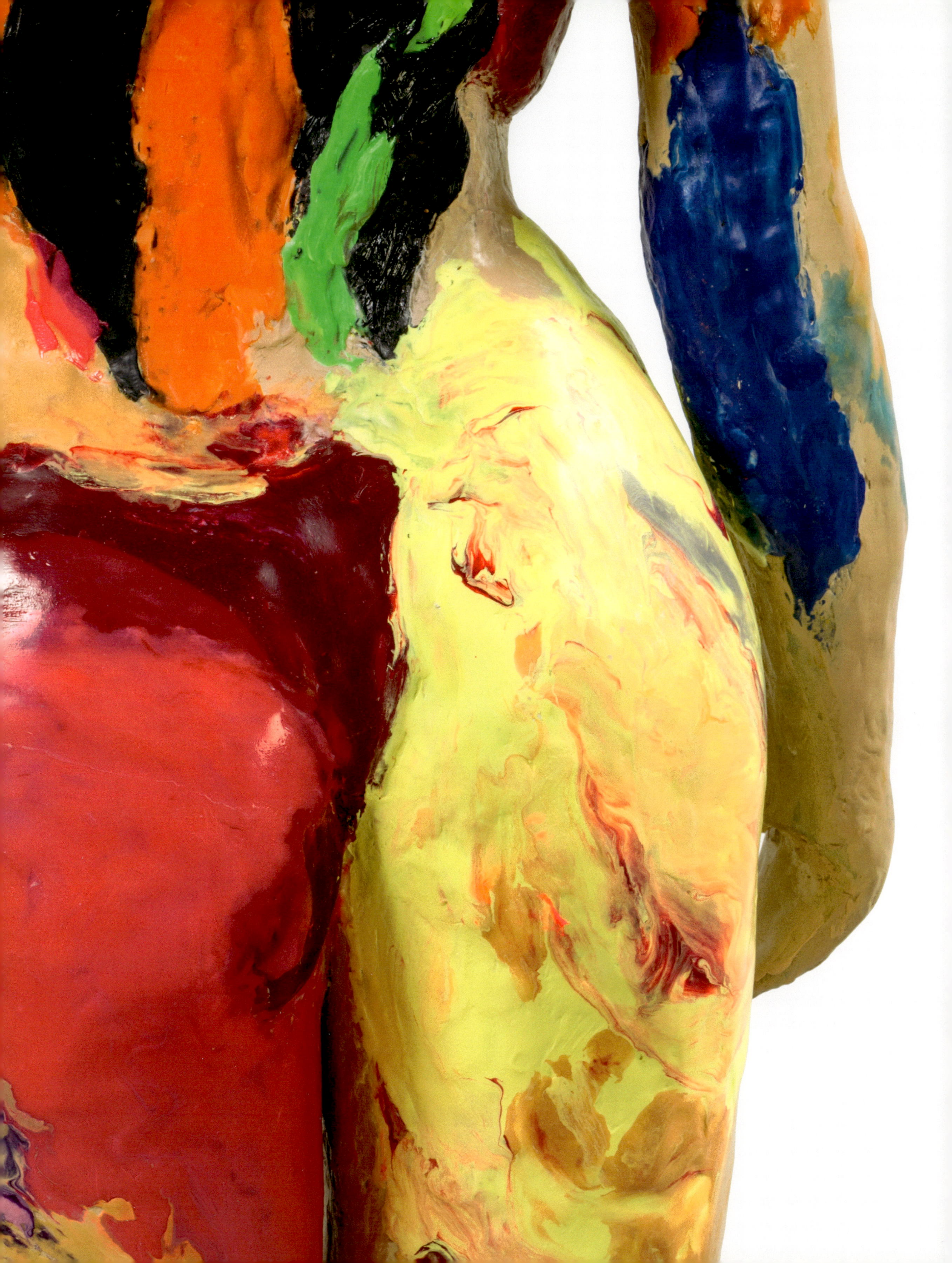

Bandleader

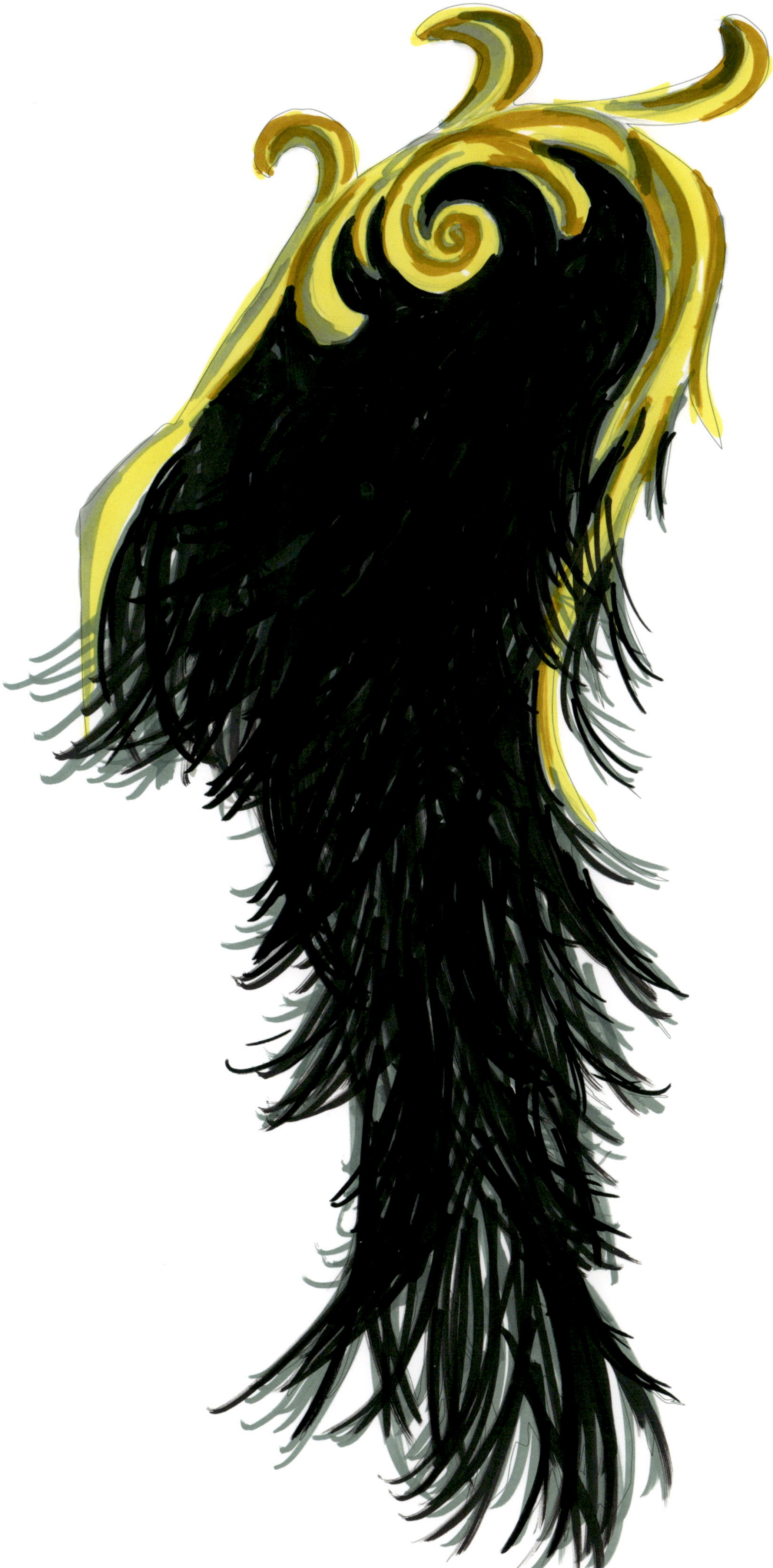

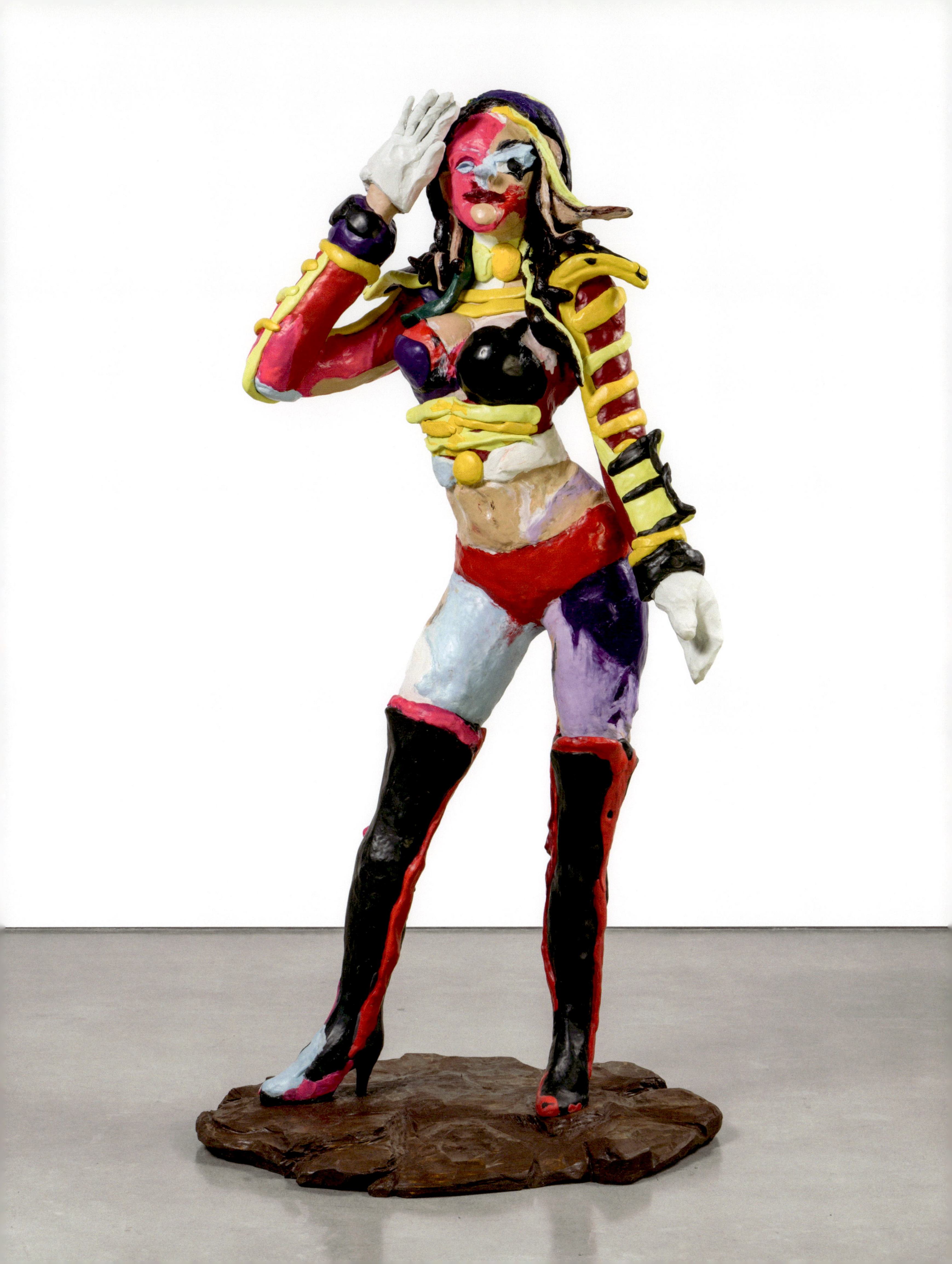

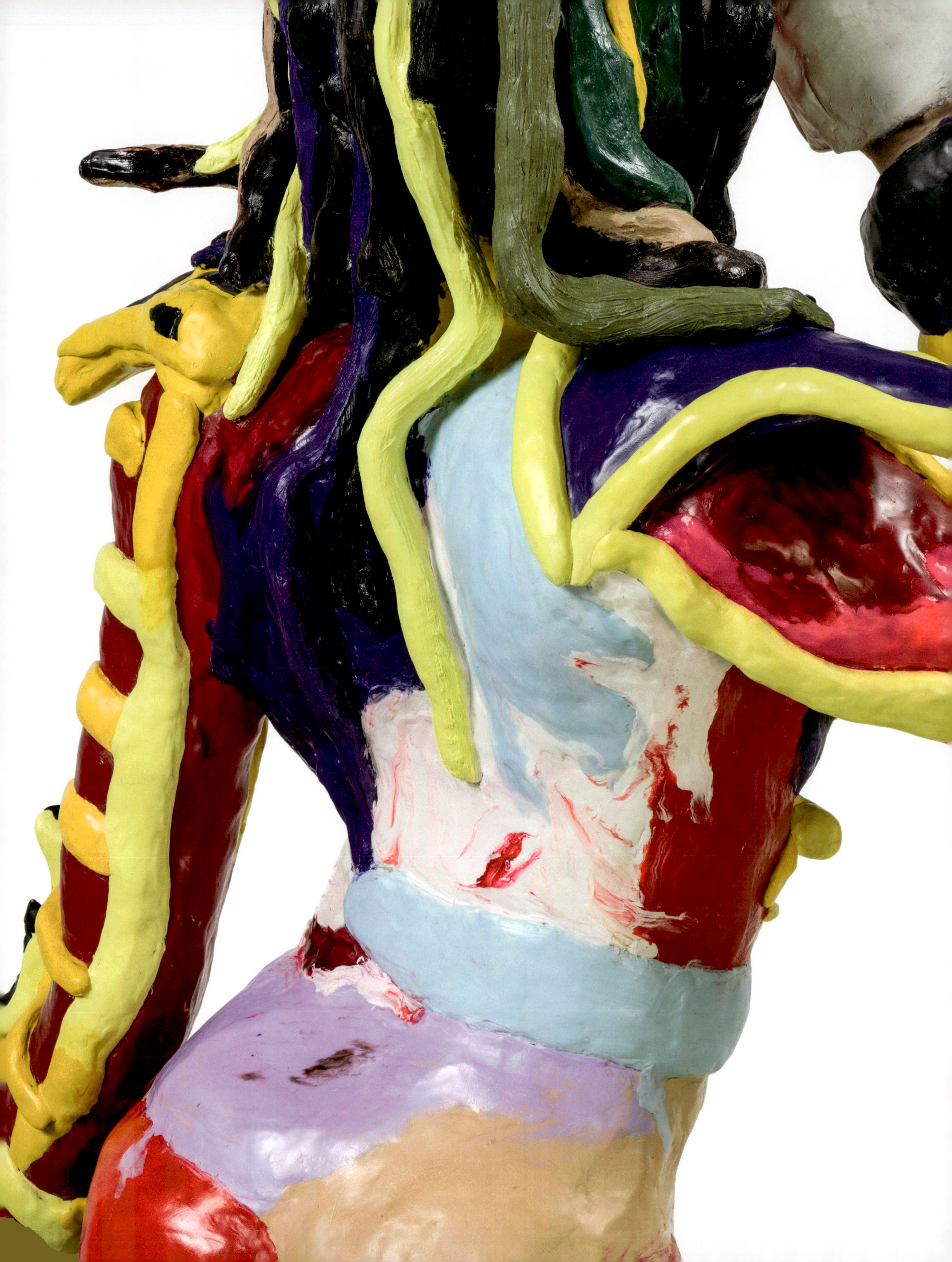

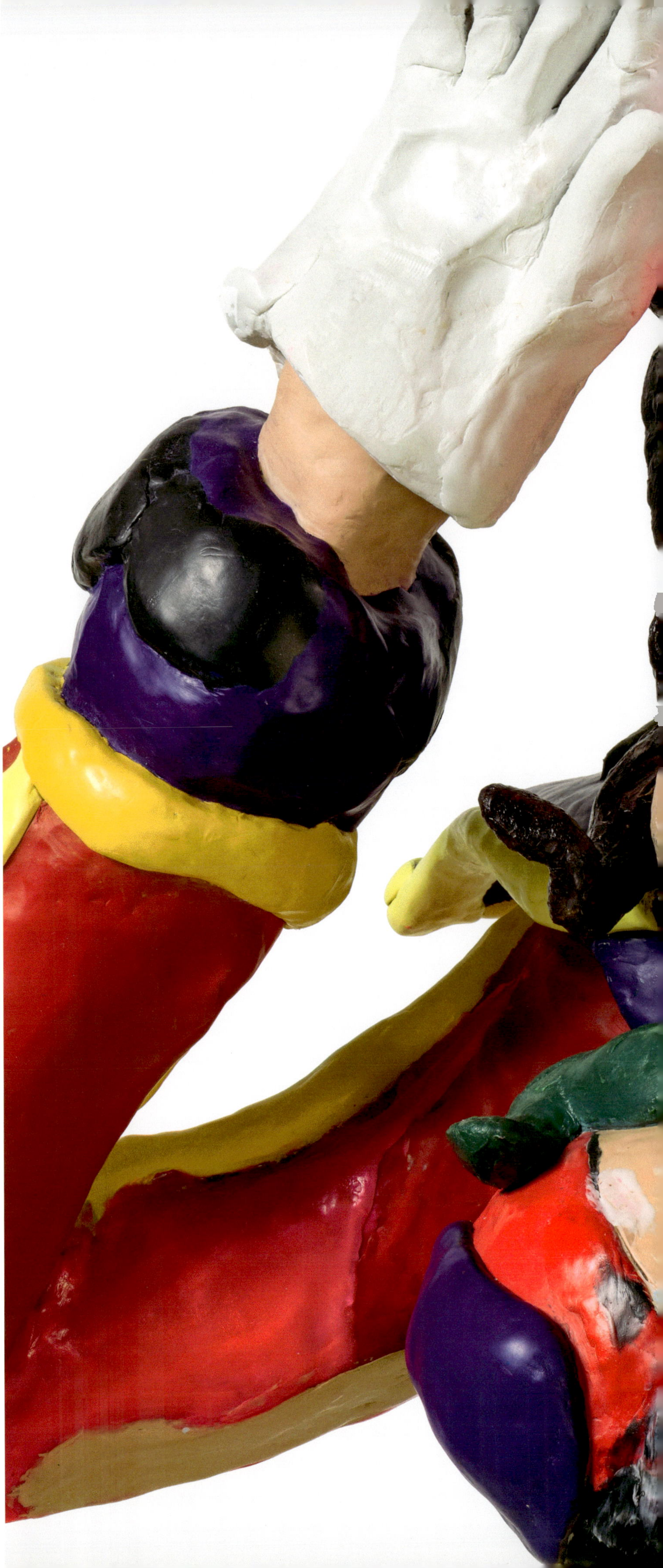

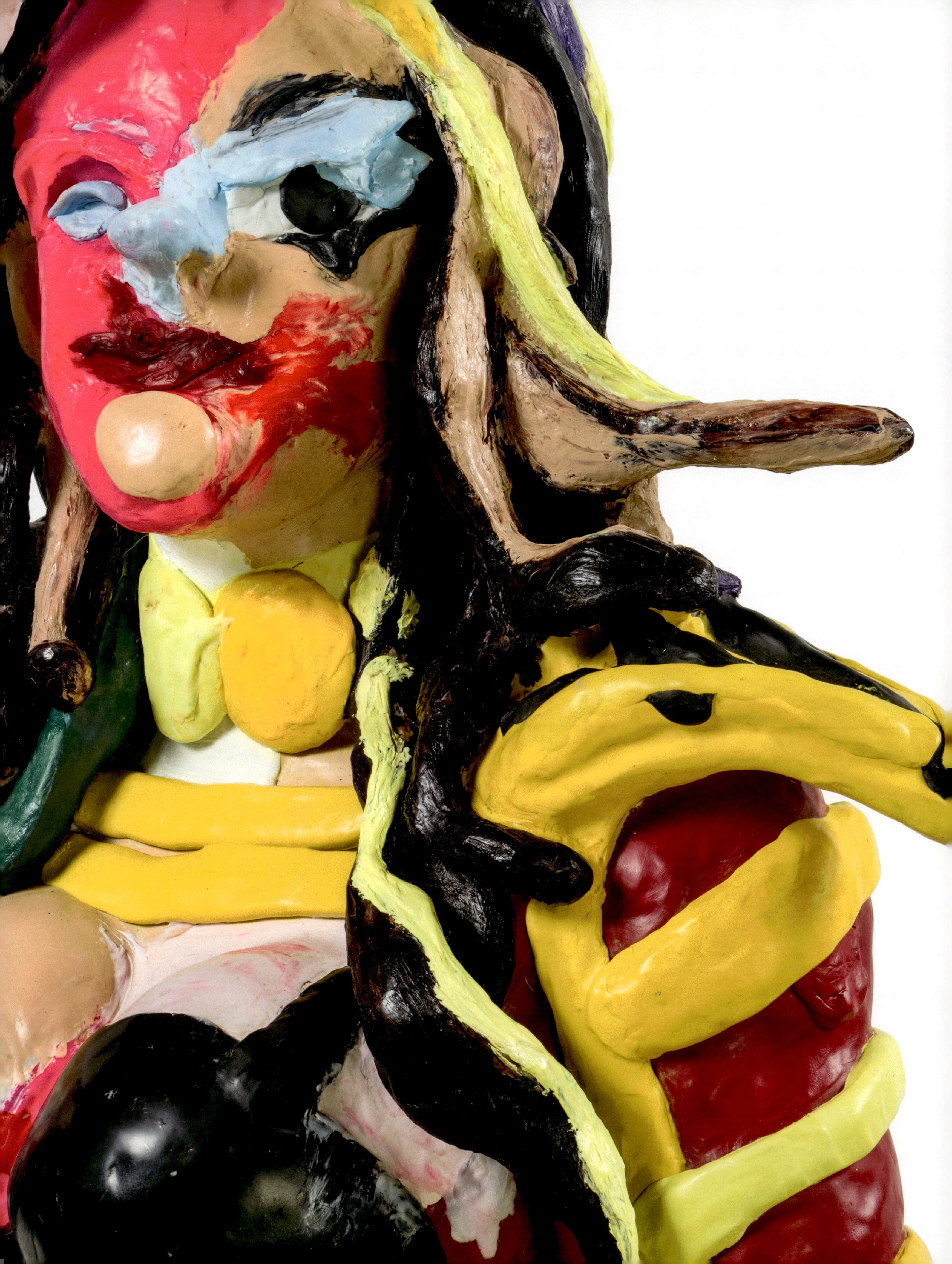

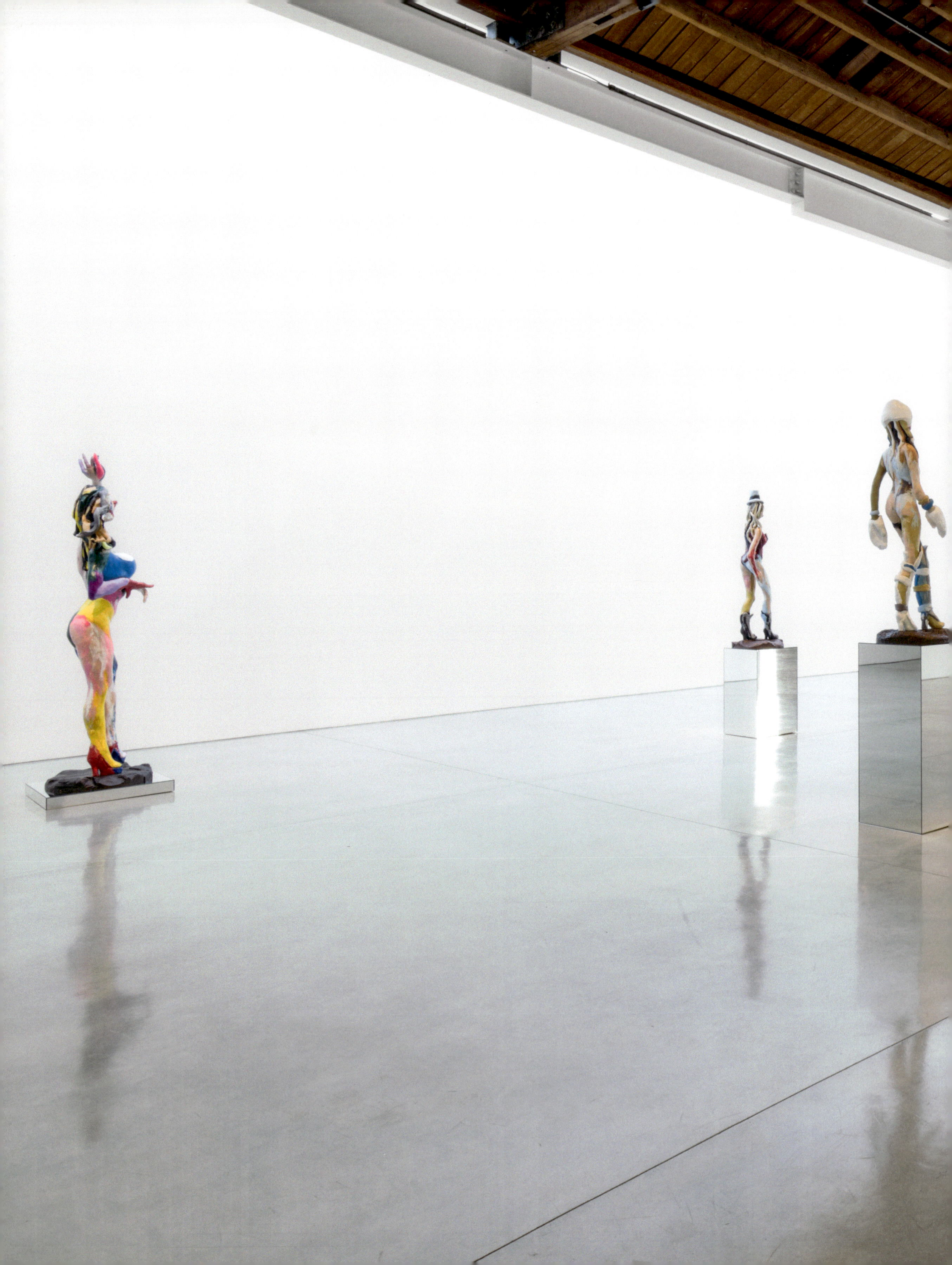

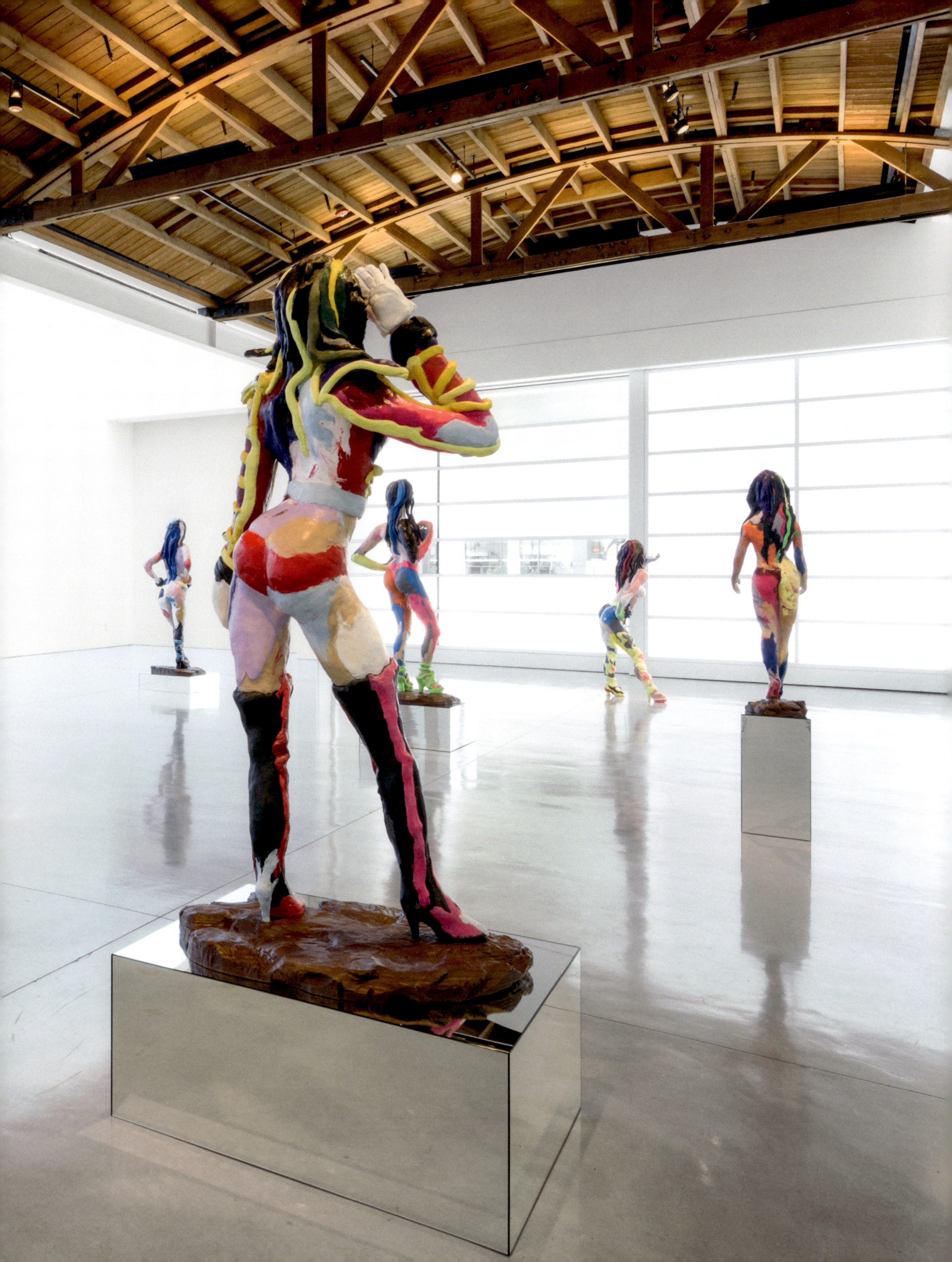

Icicles

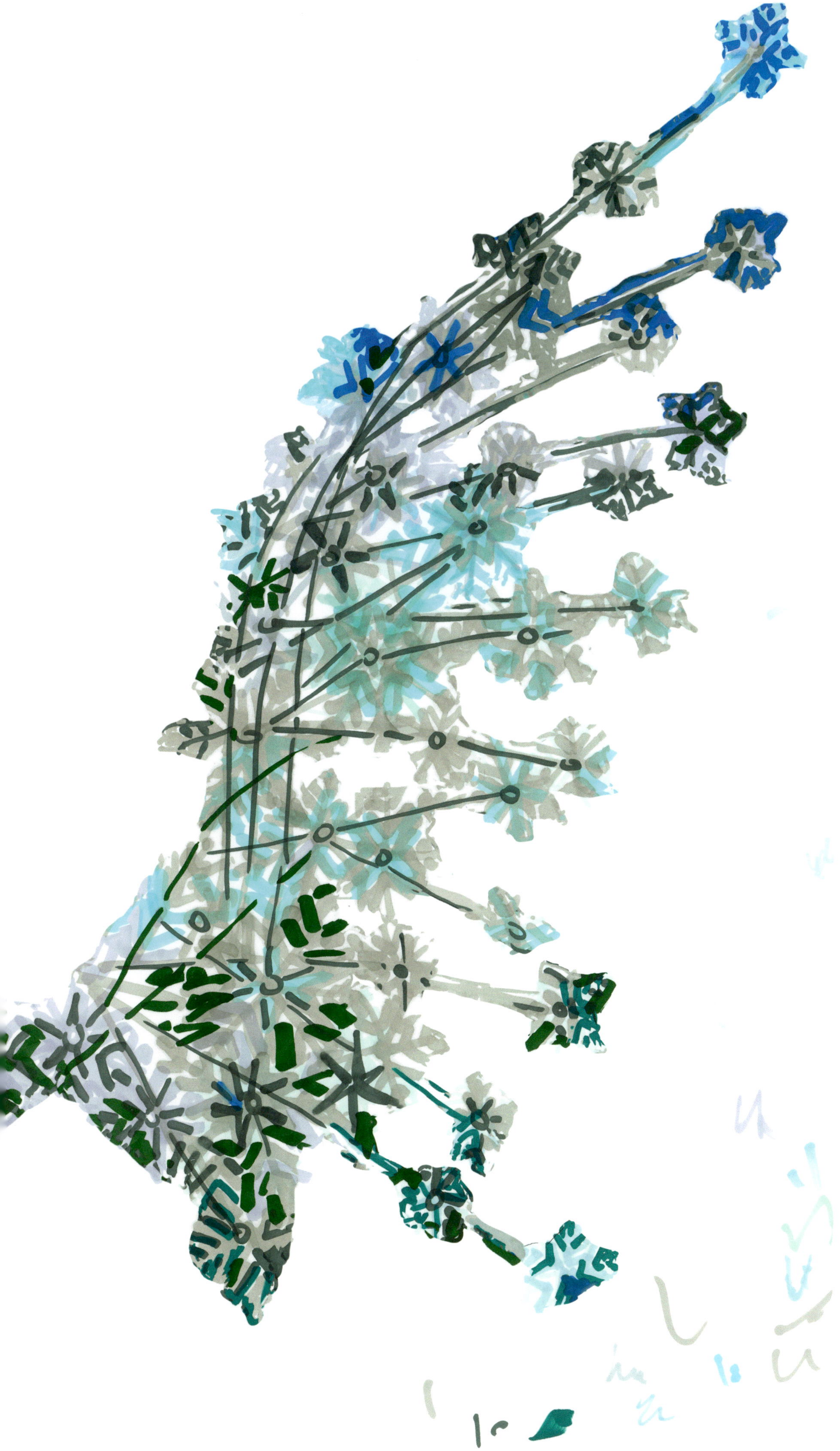

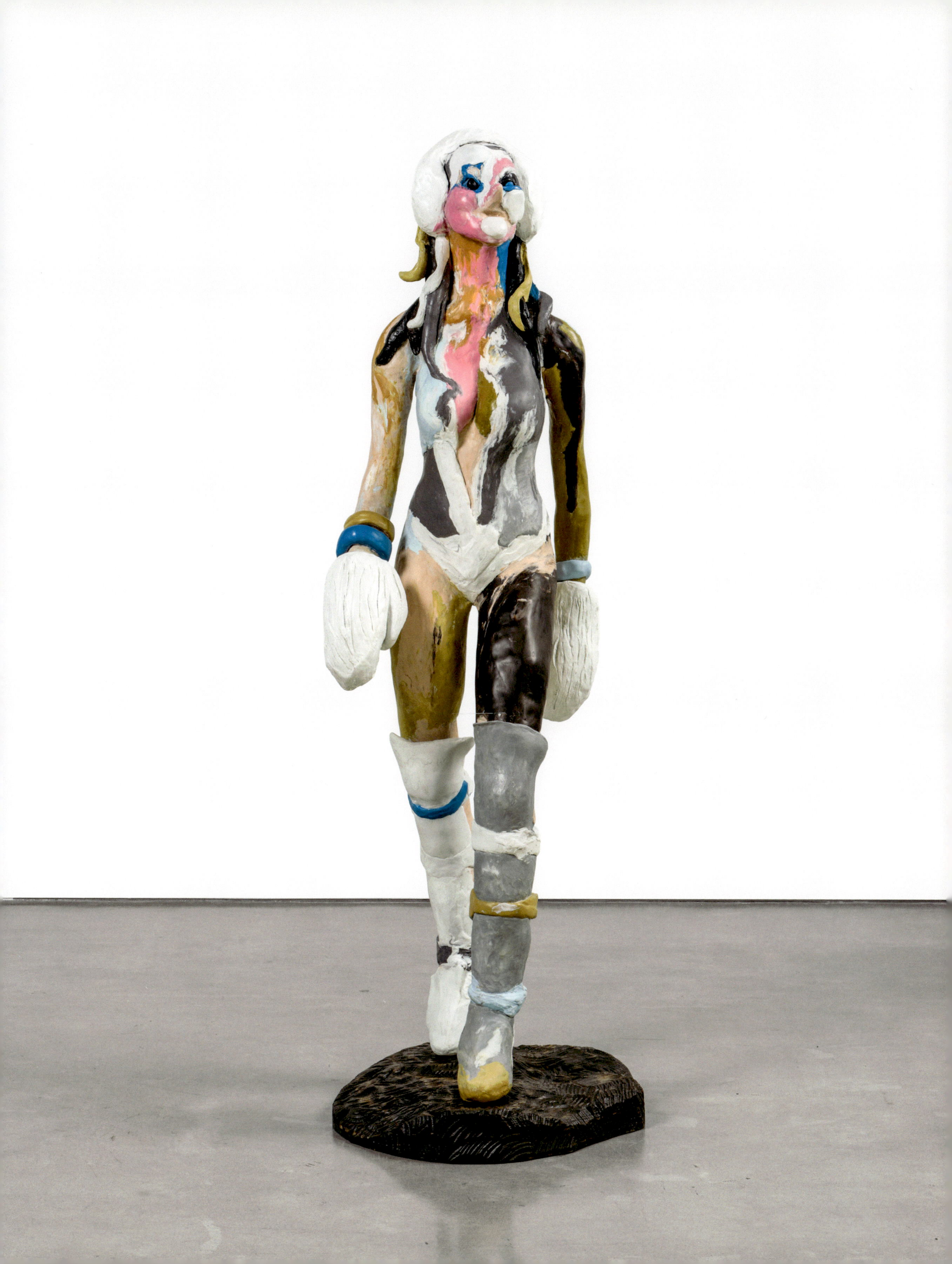

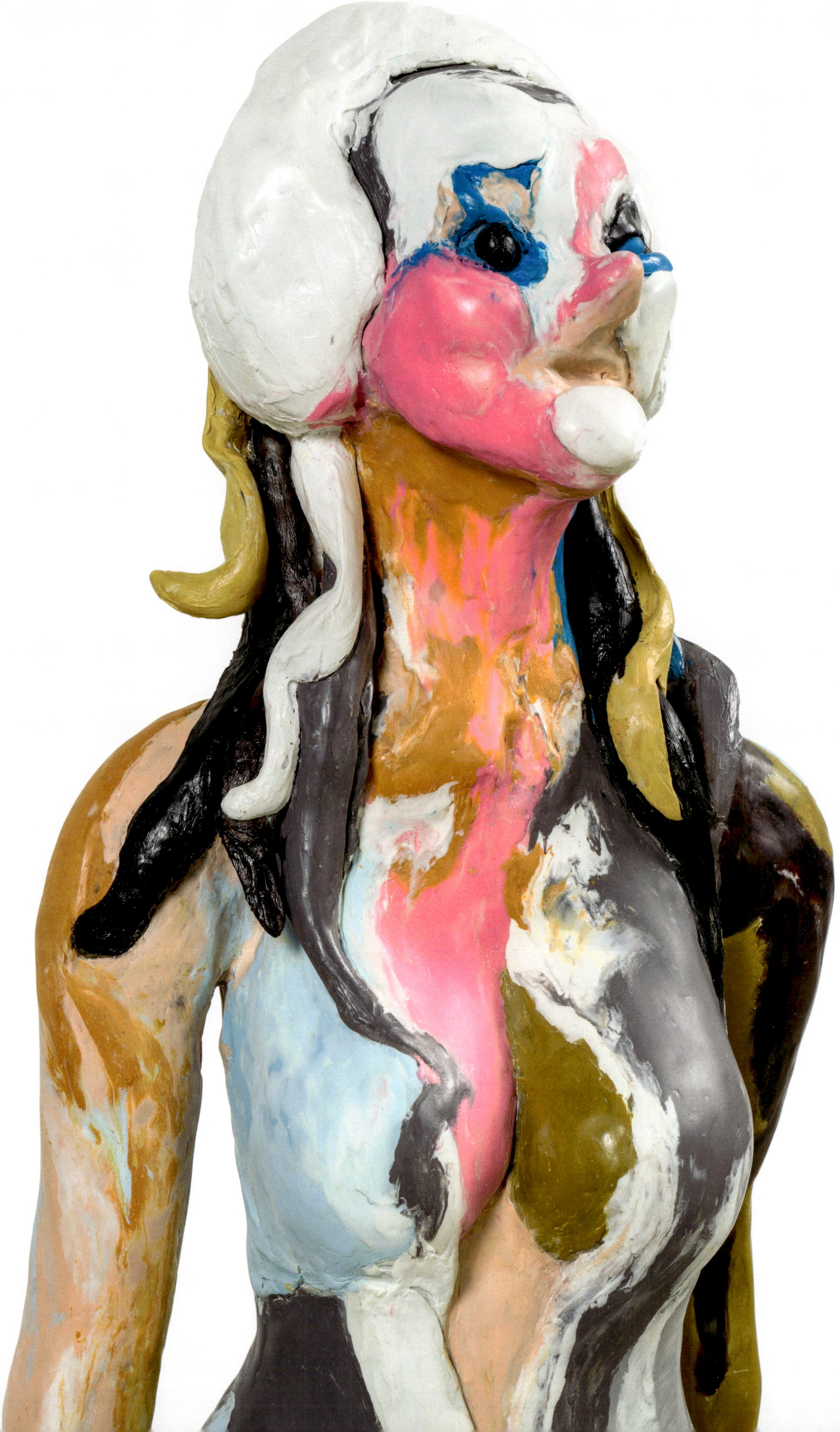

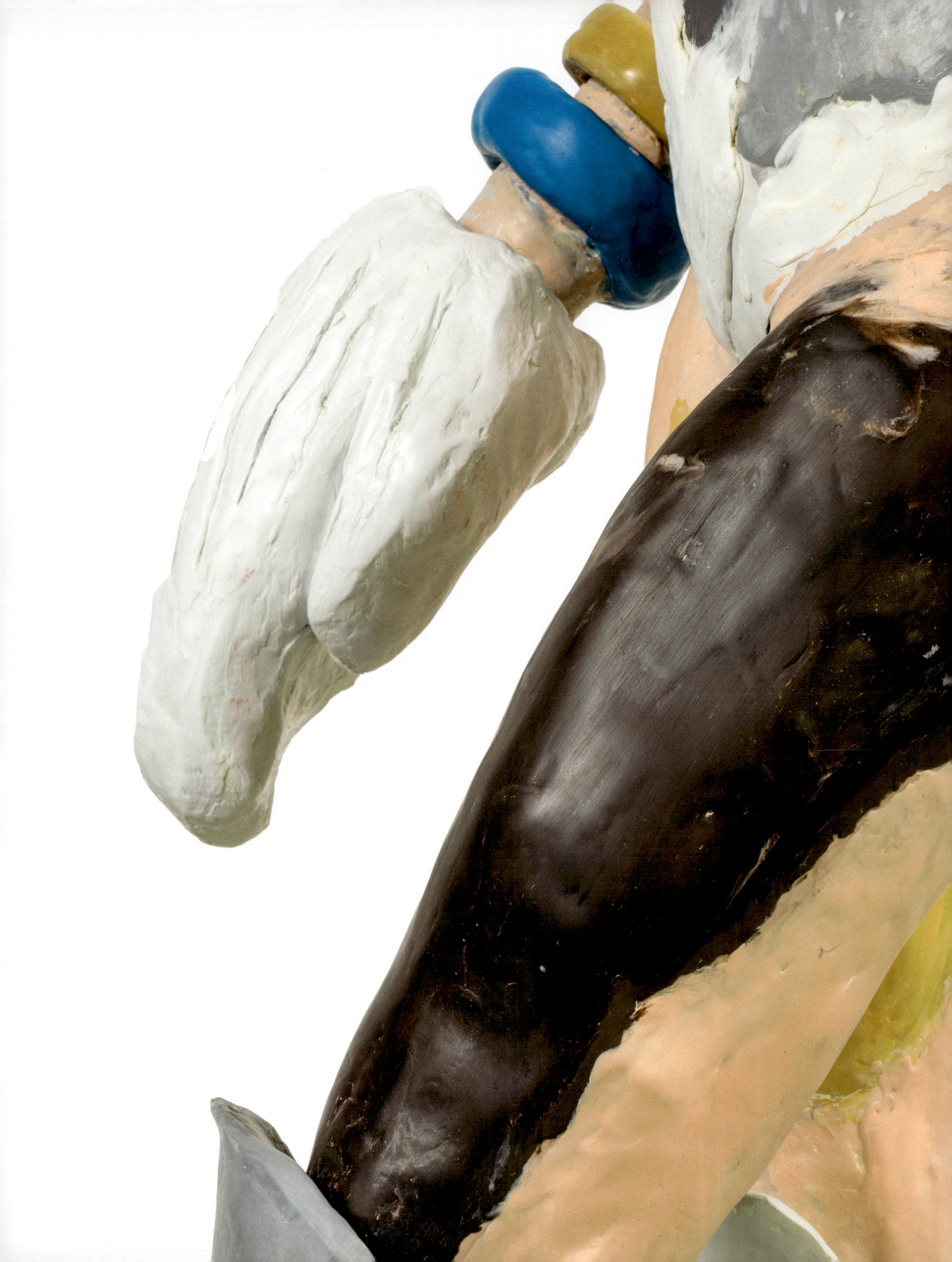

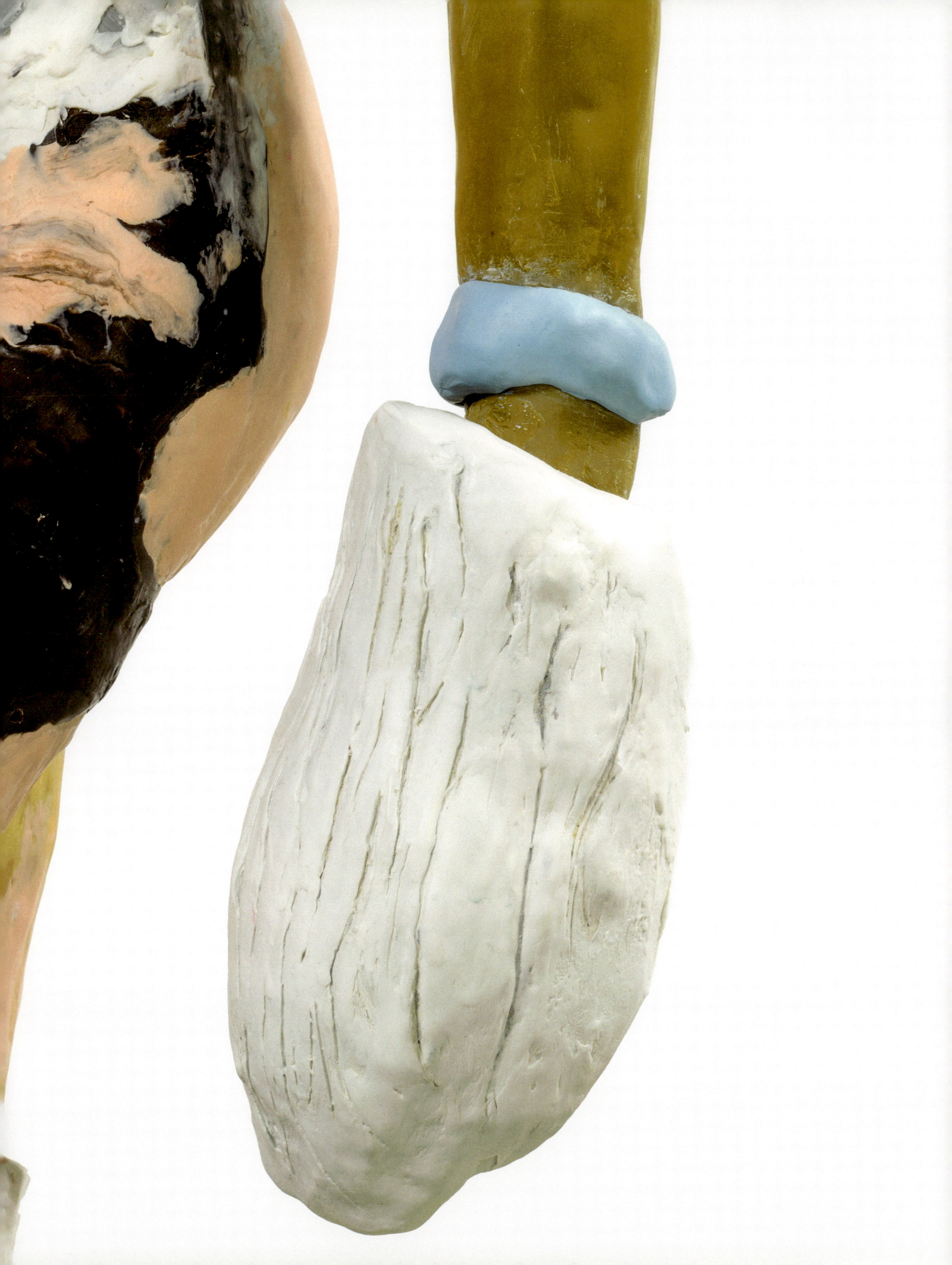

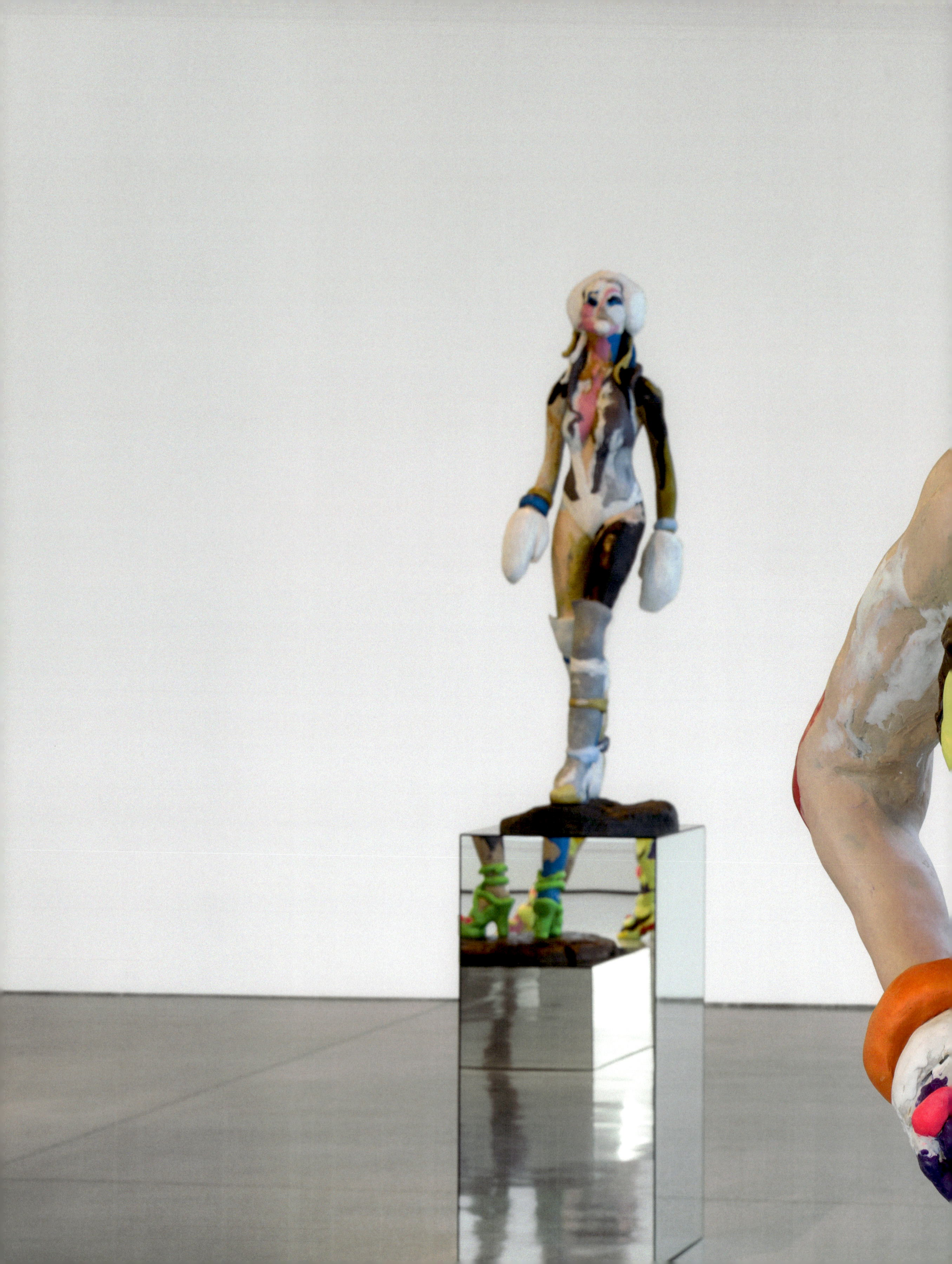

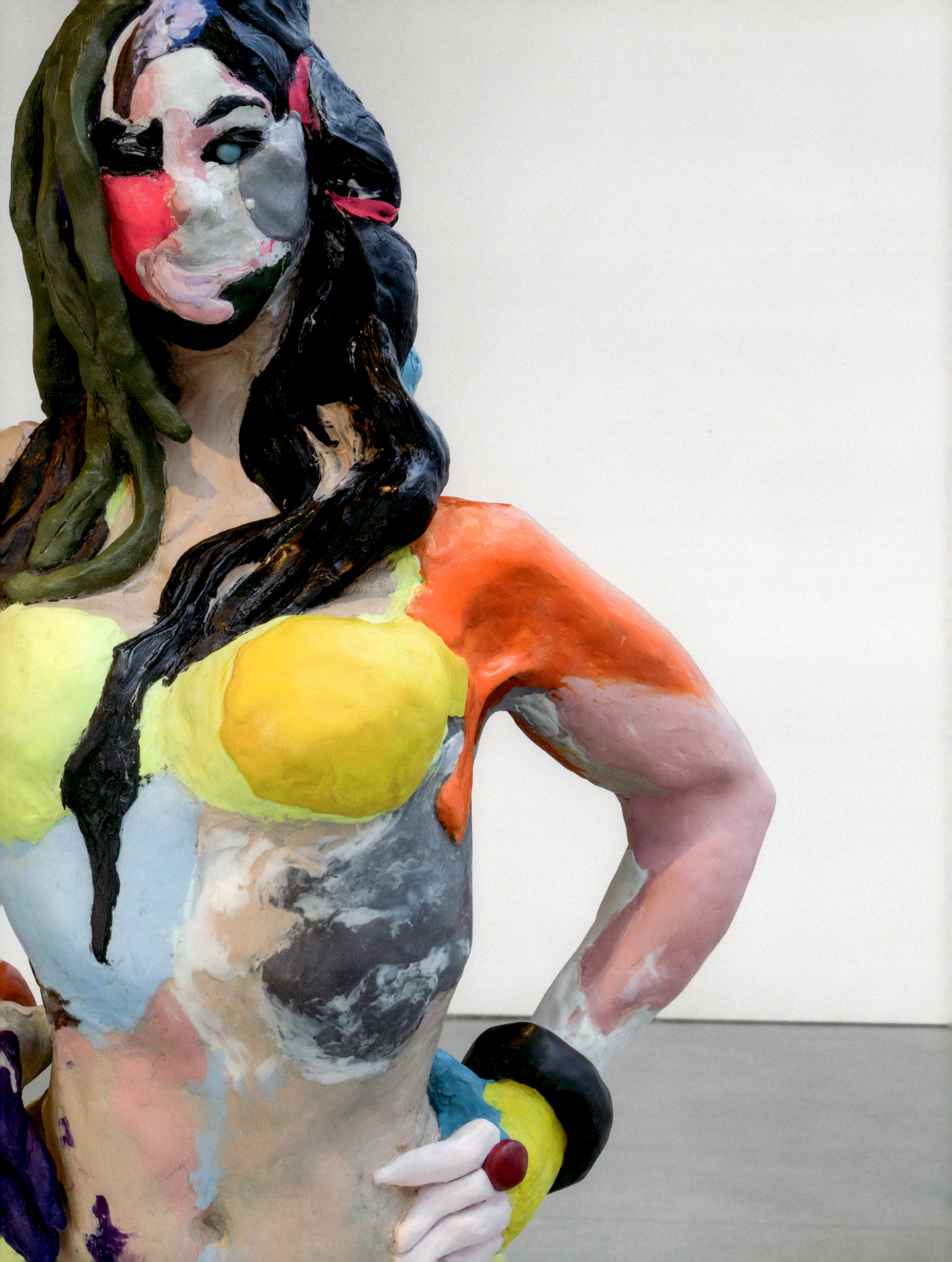

Fireworks

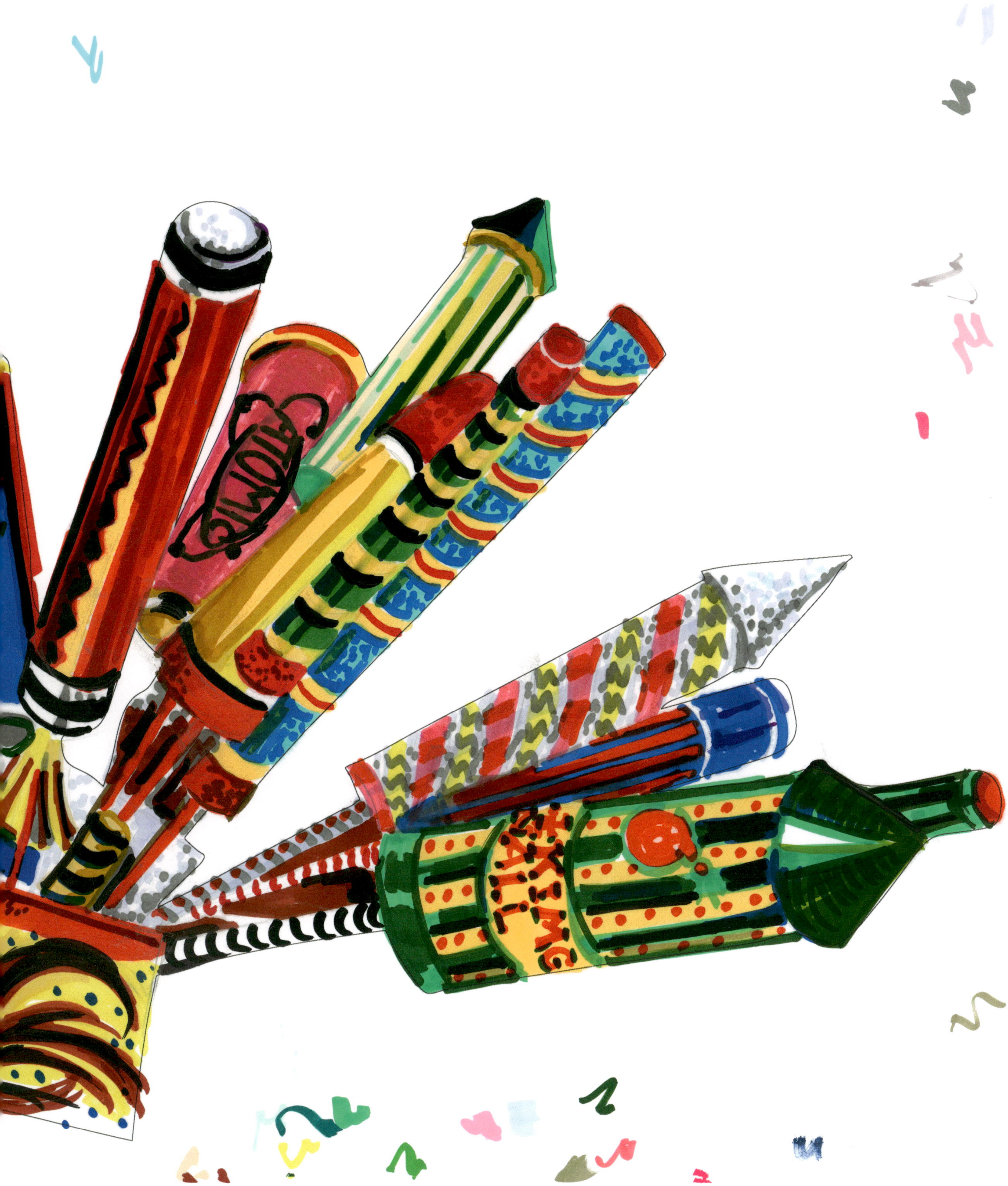

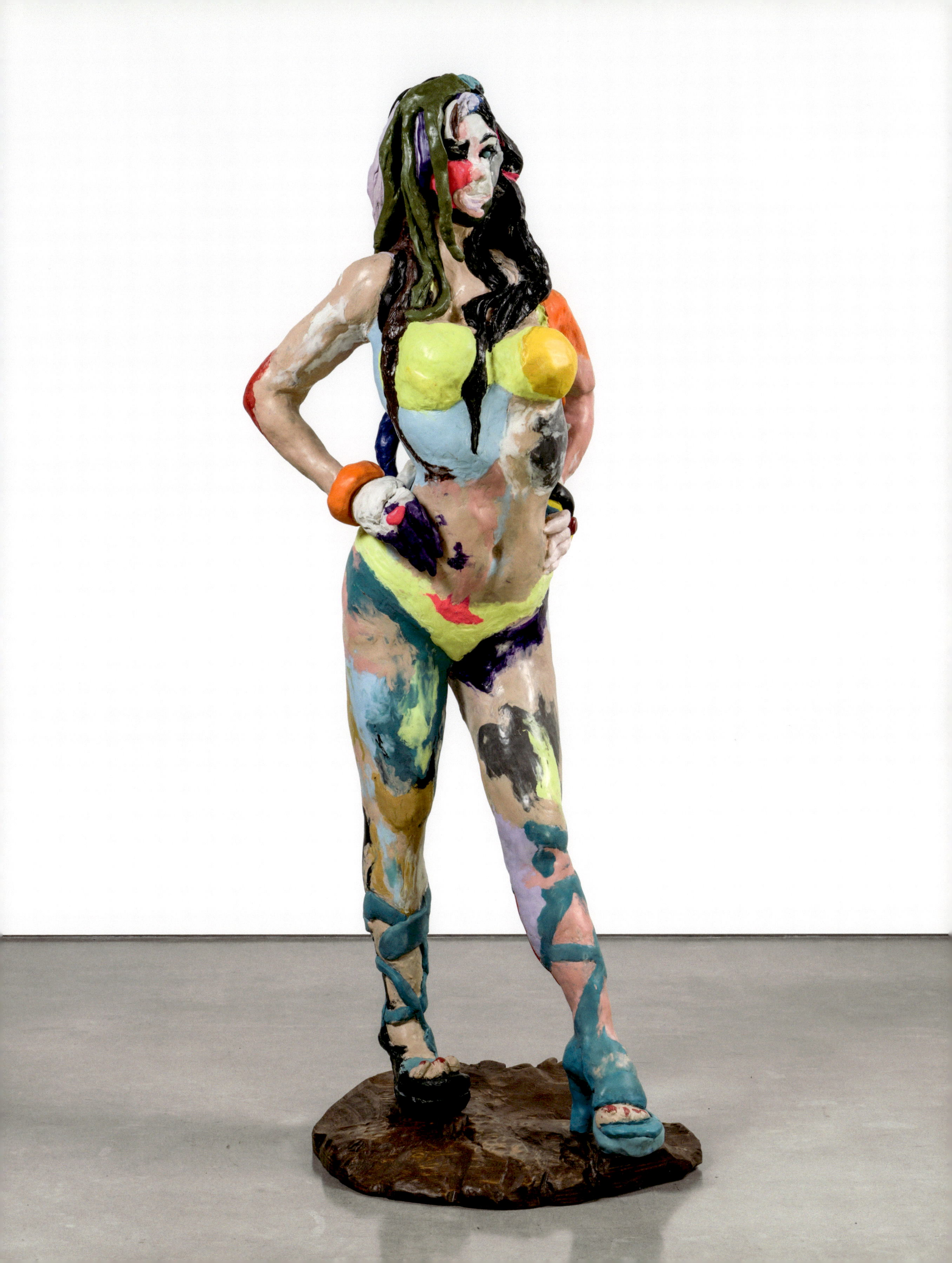

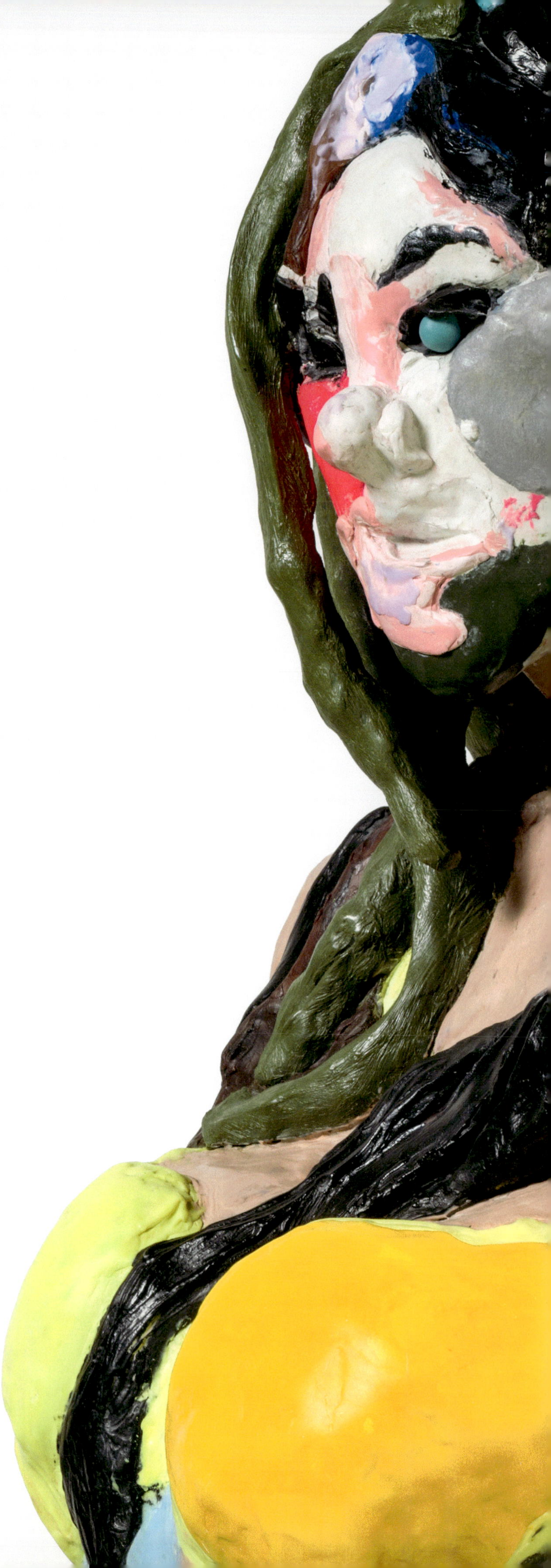

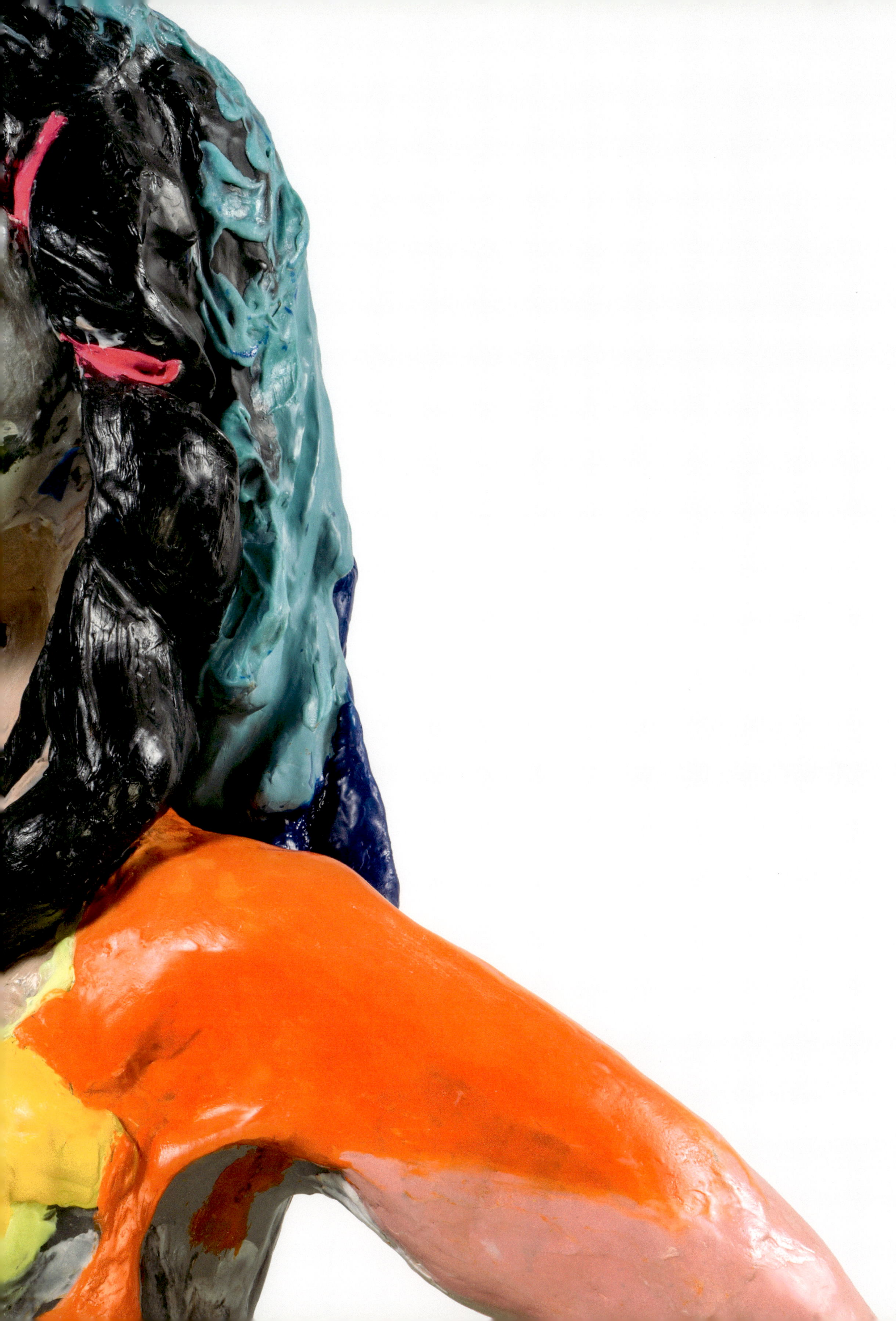

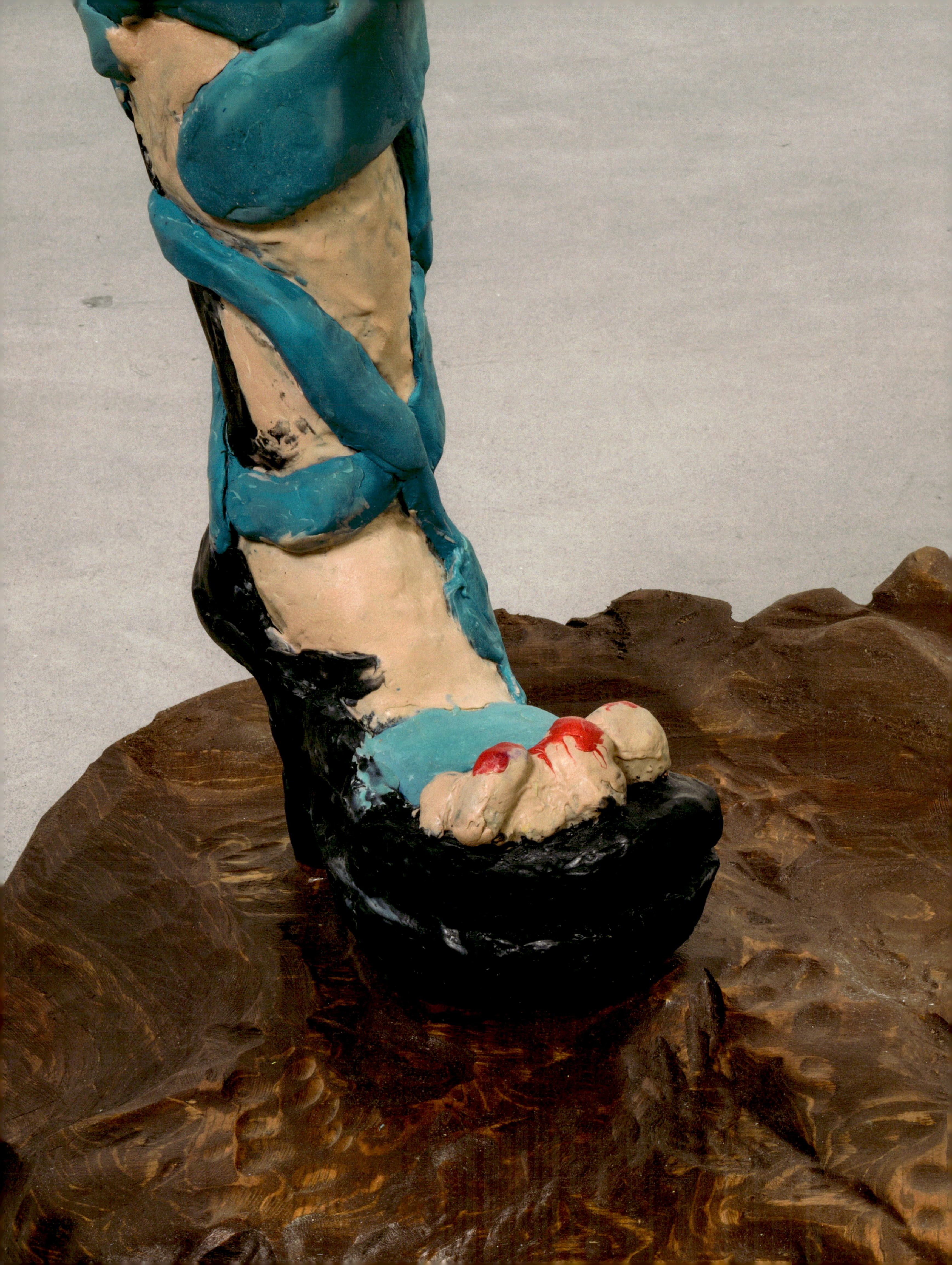

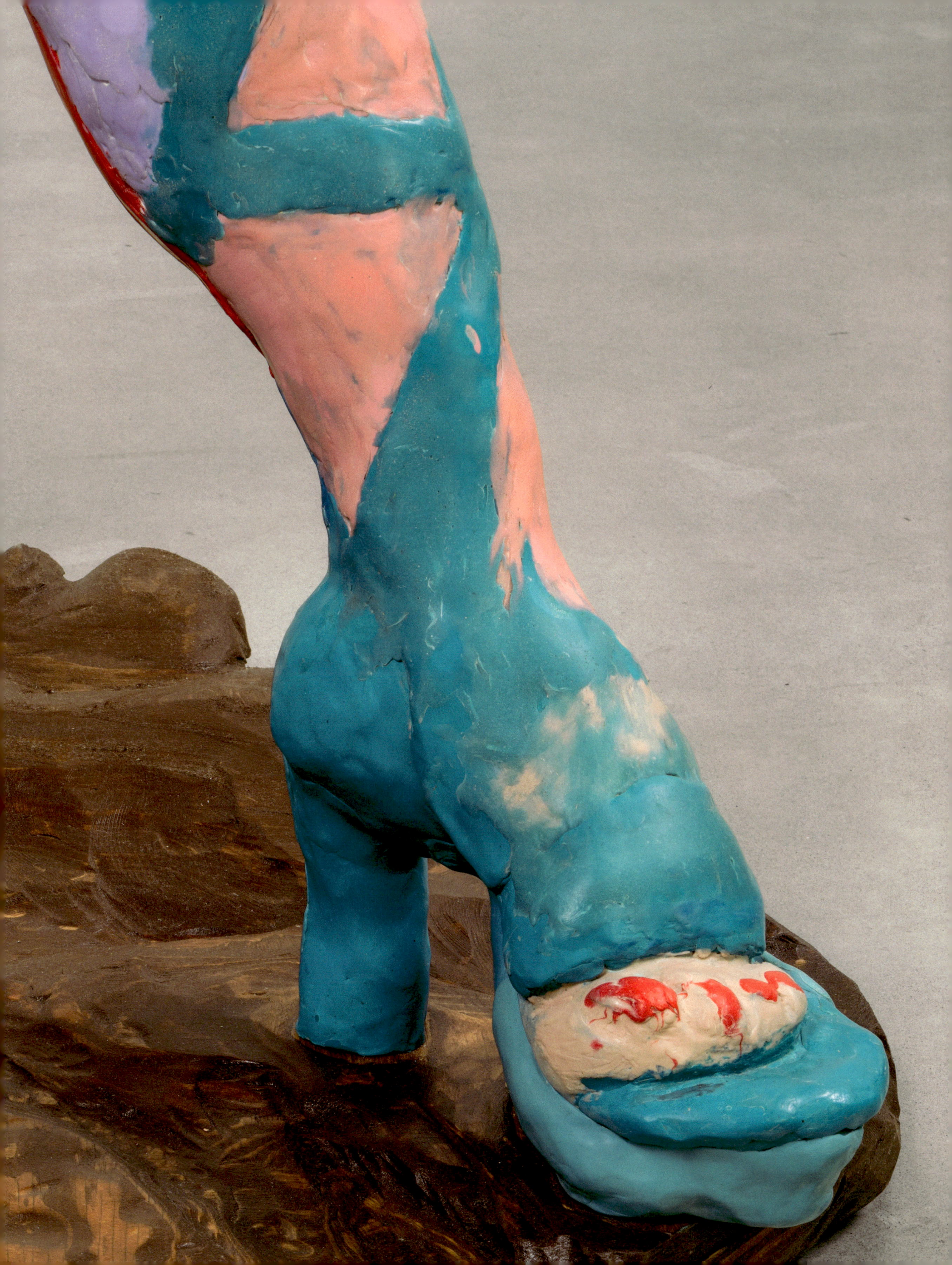

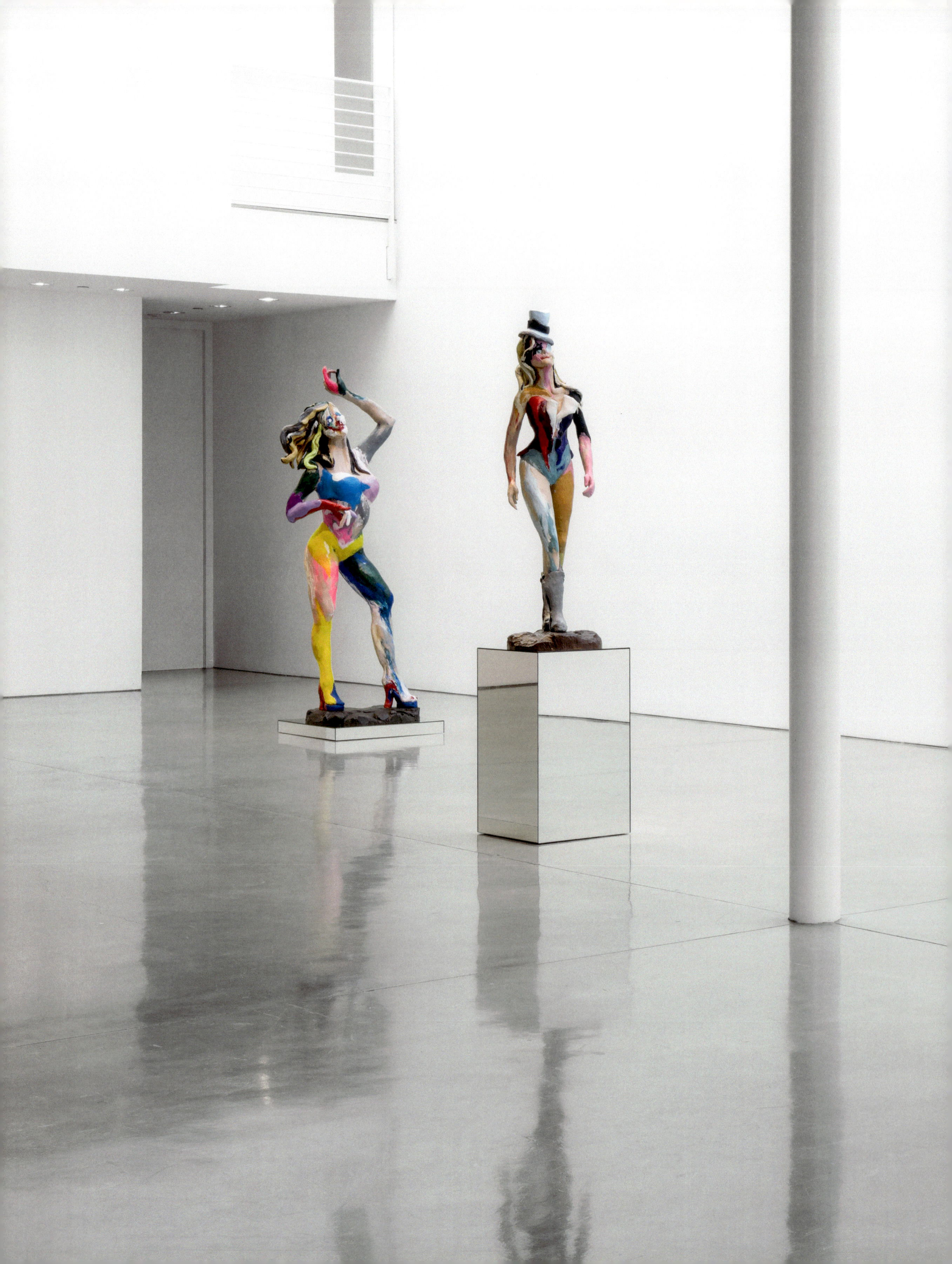

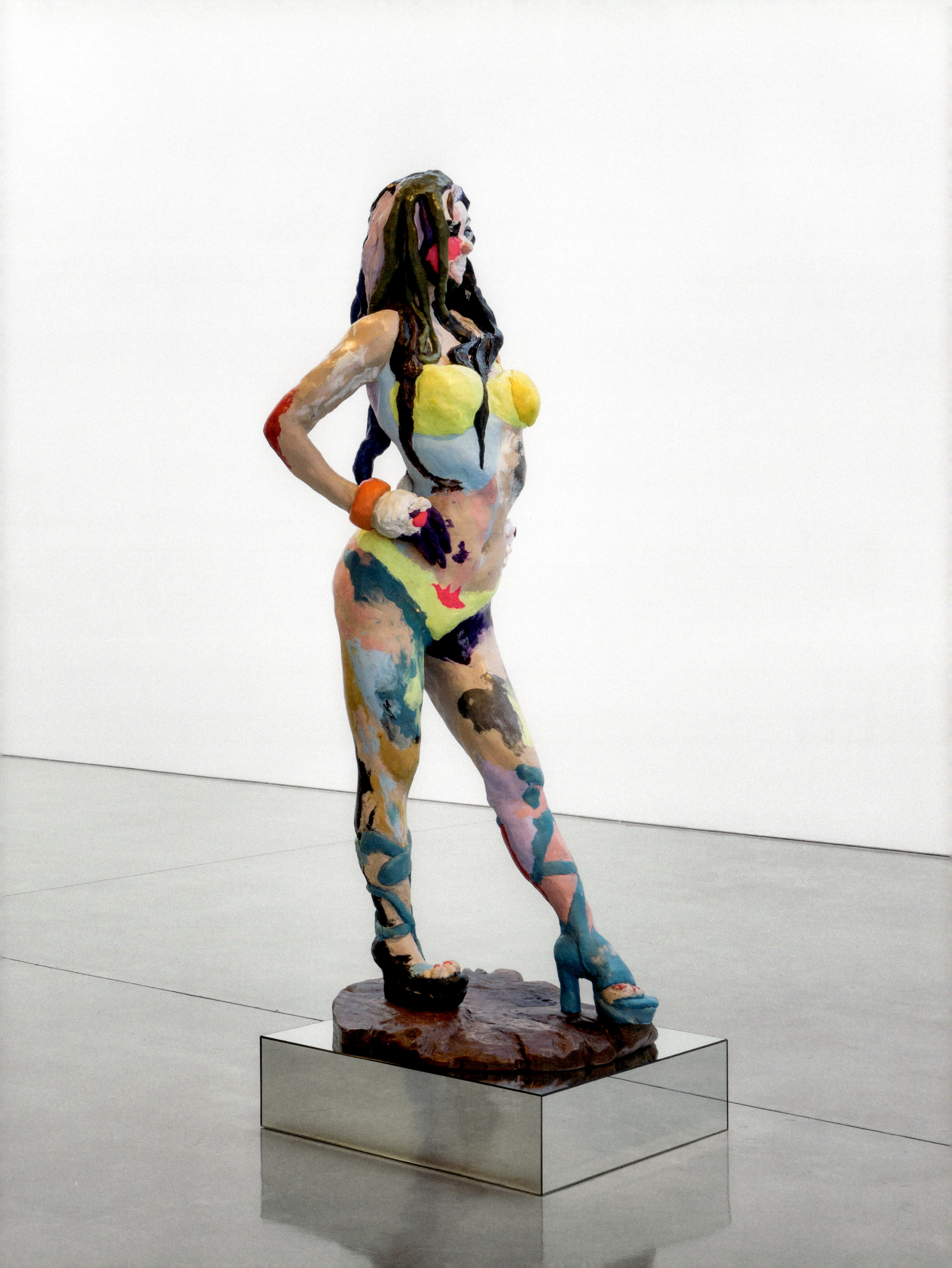

Spats

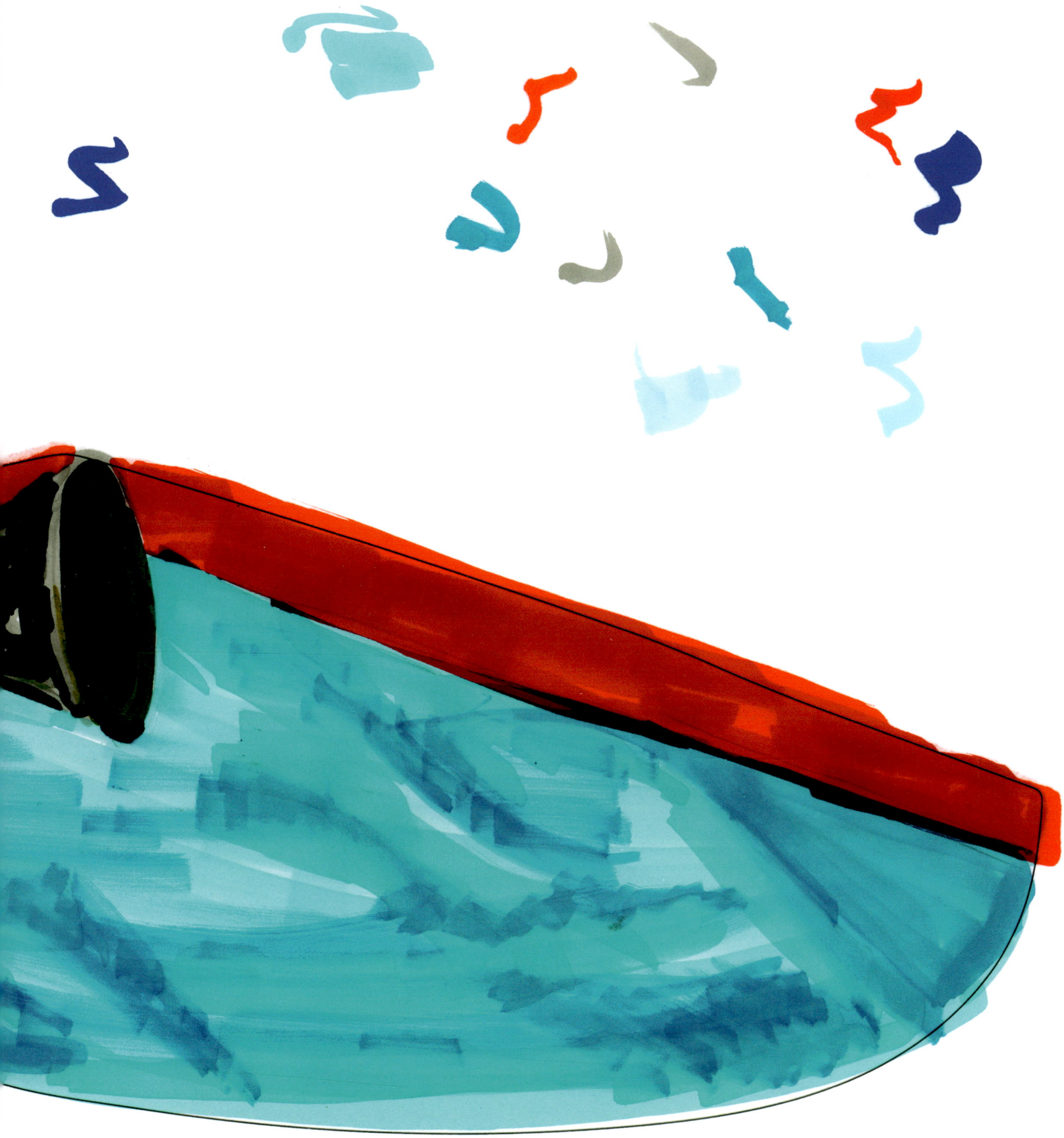

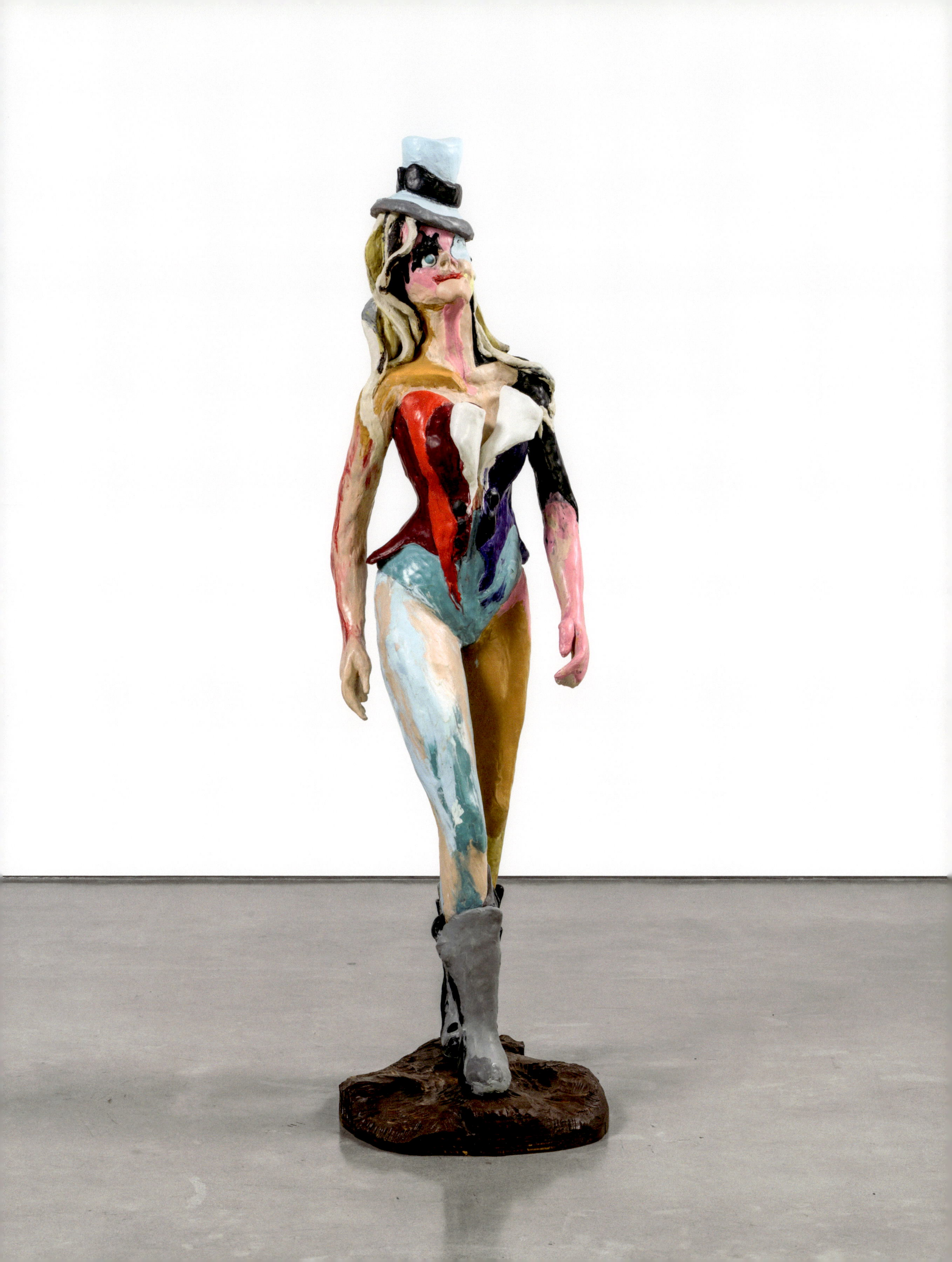

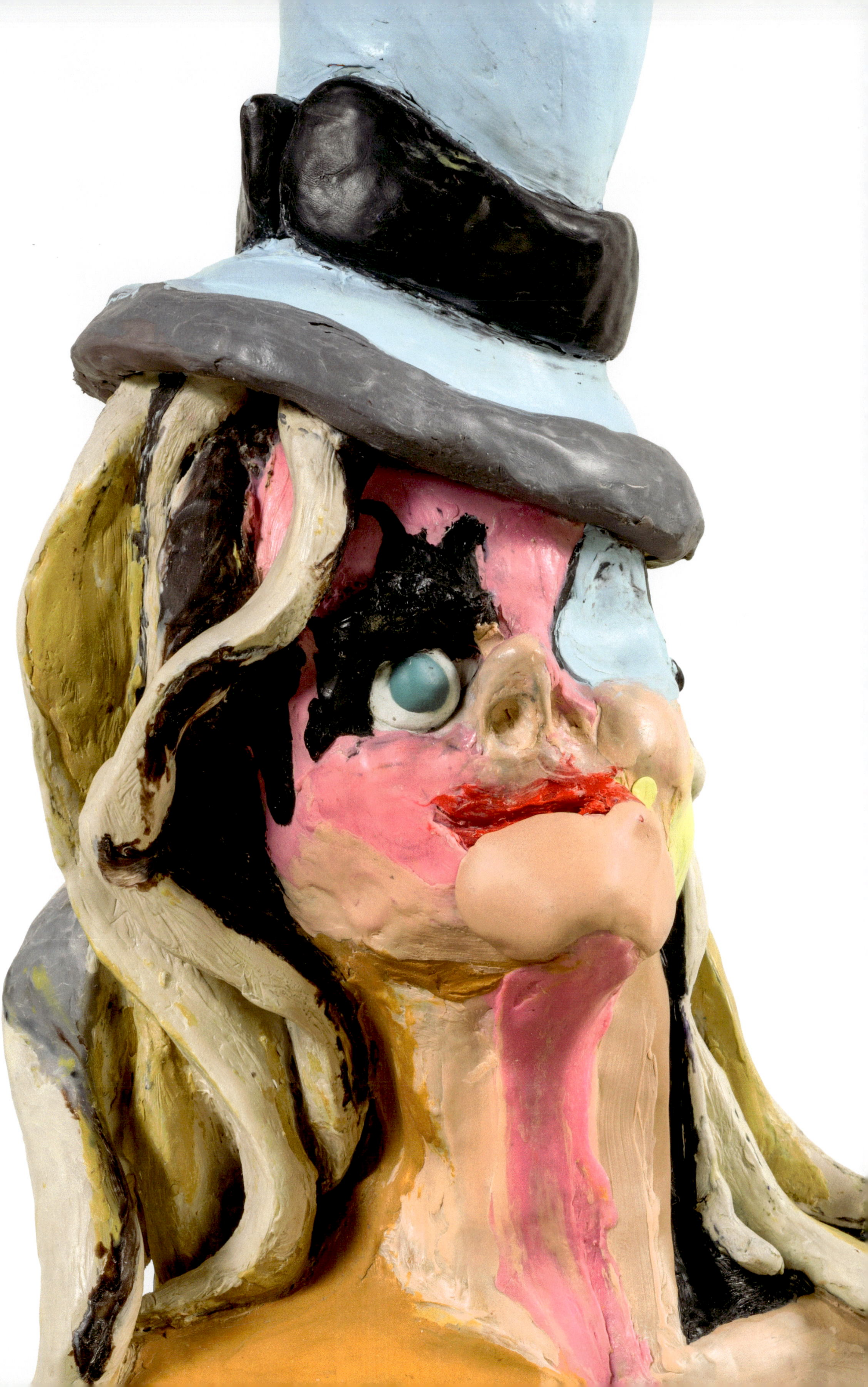

Ballerina

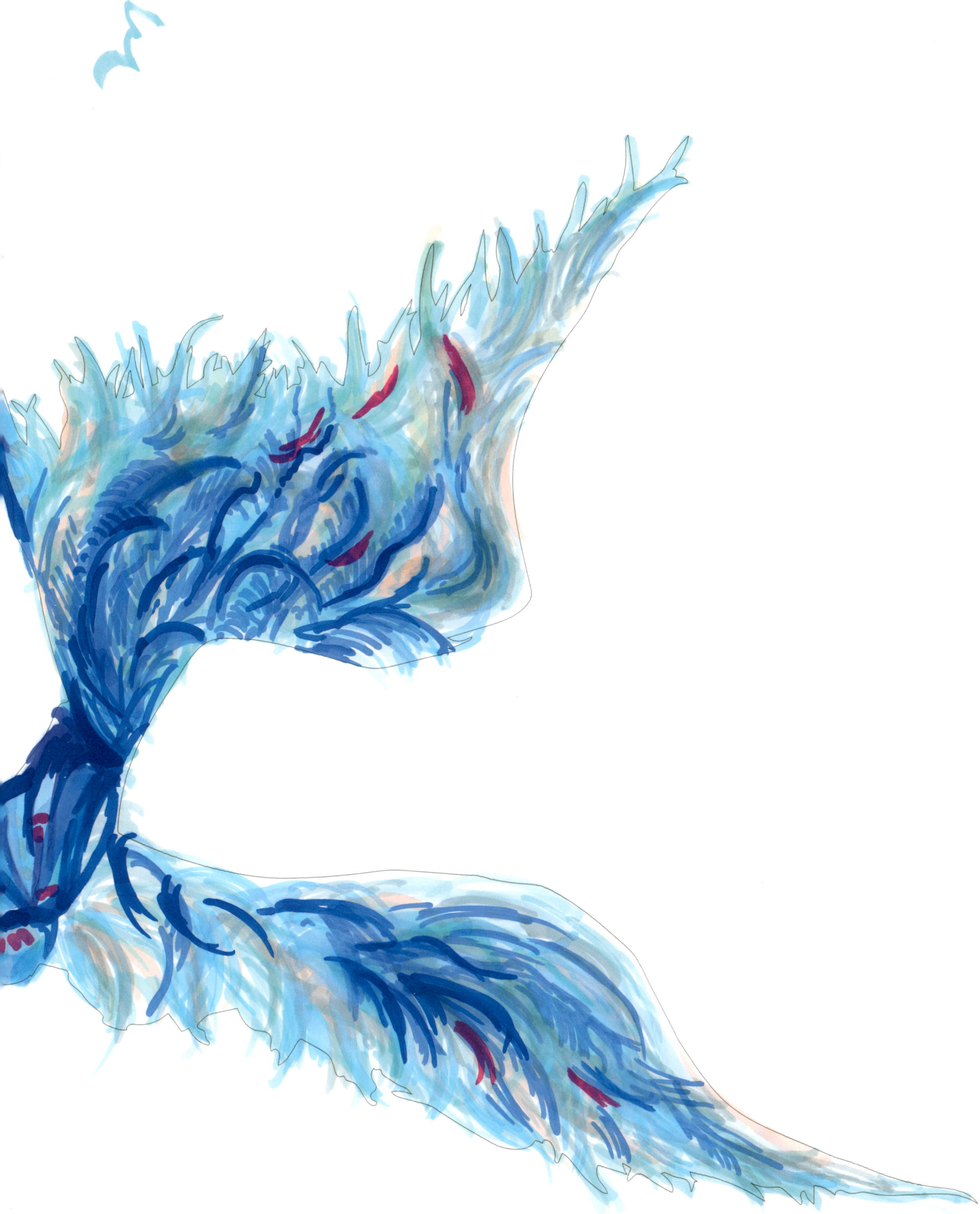

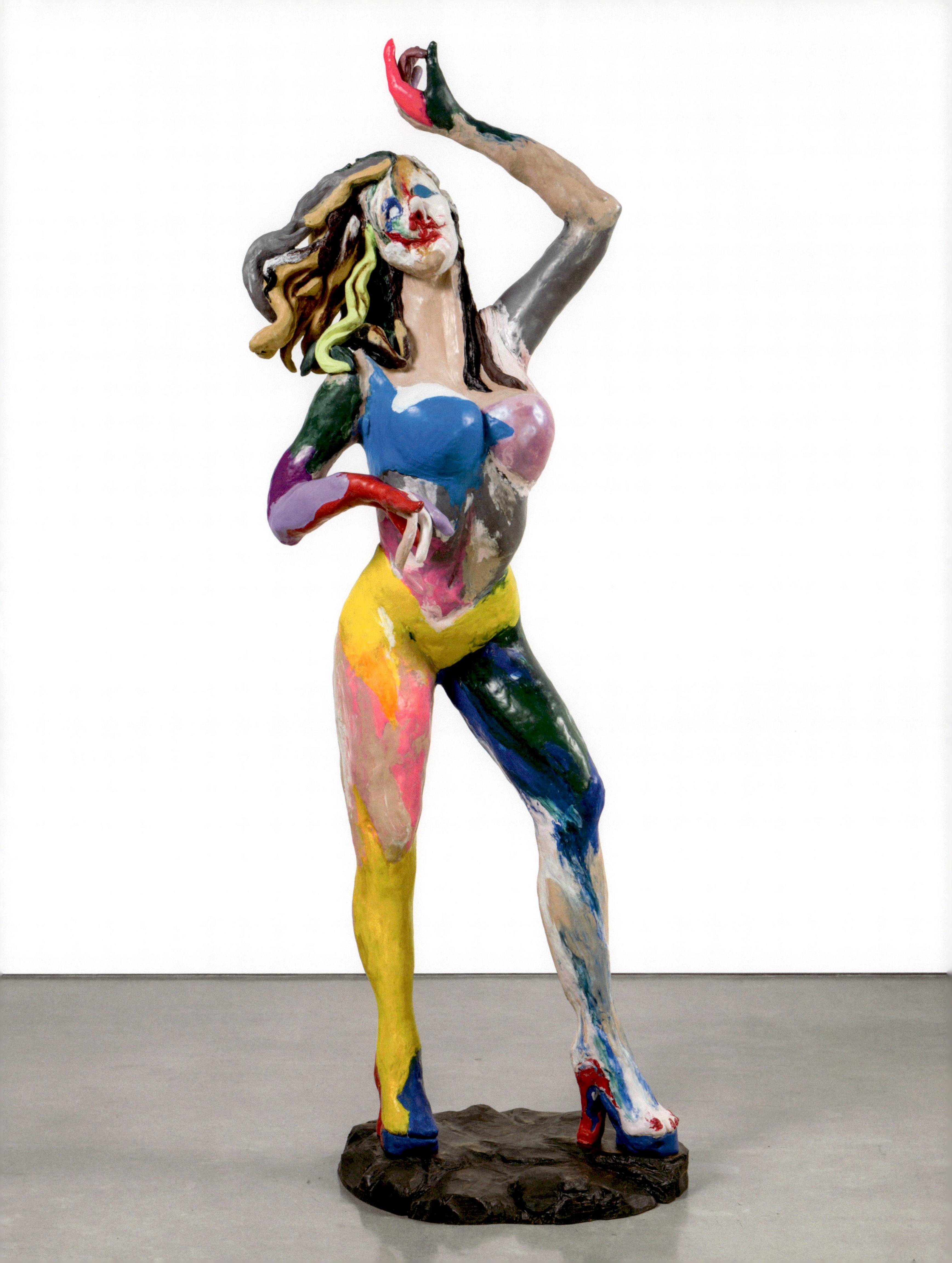

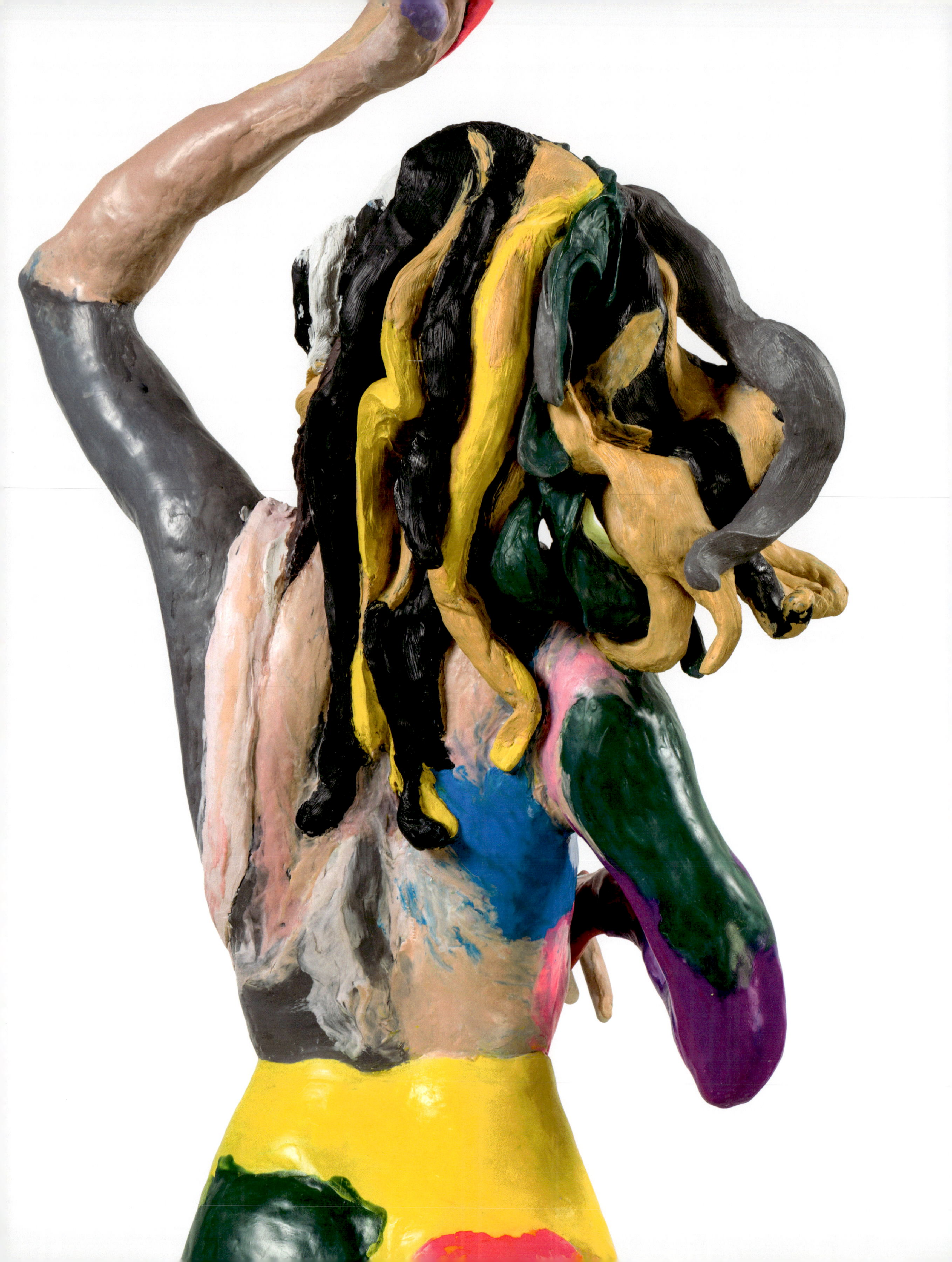

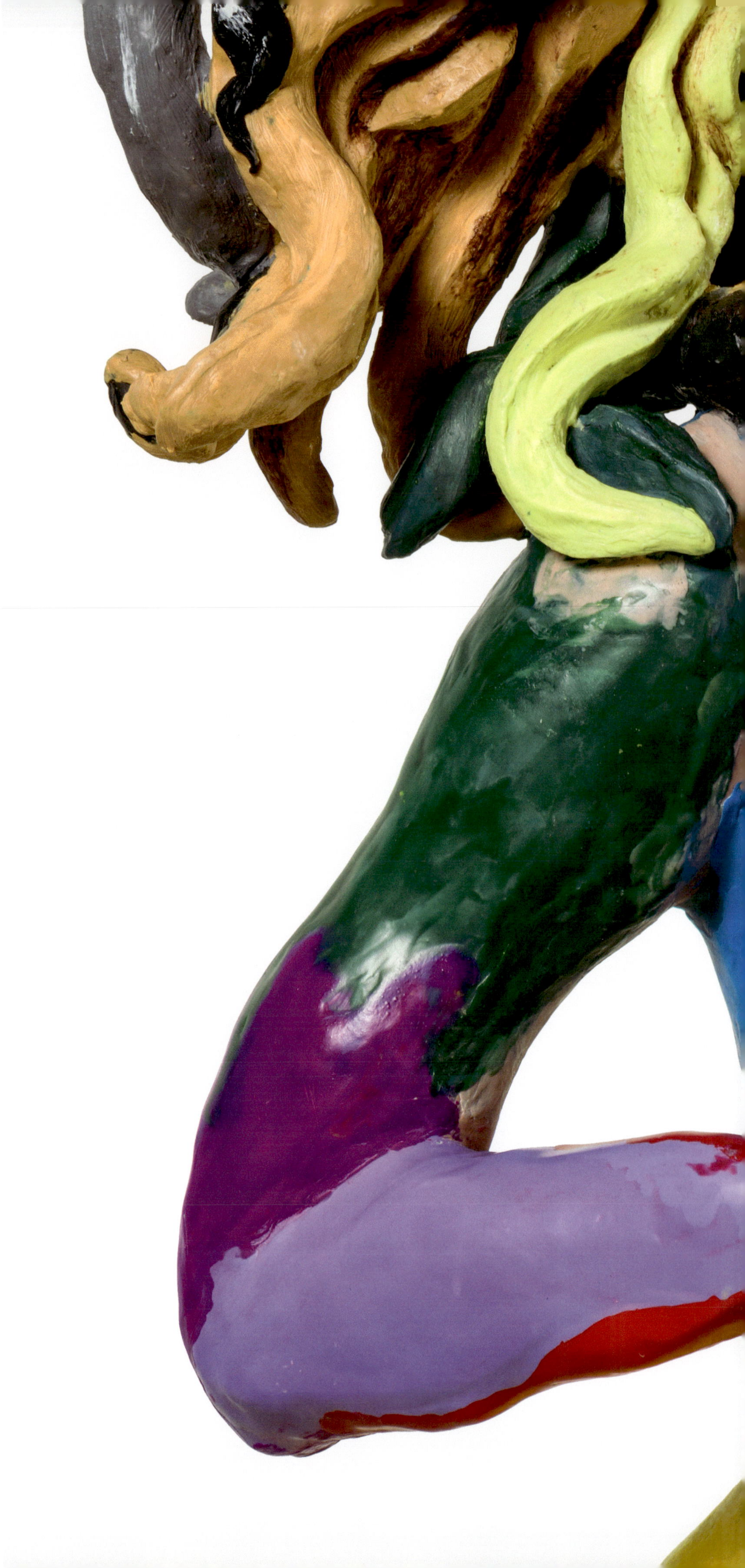

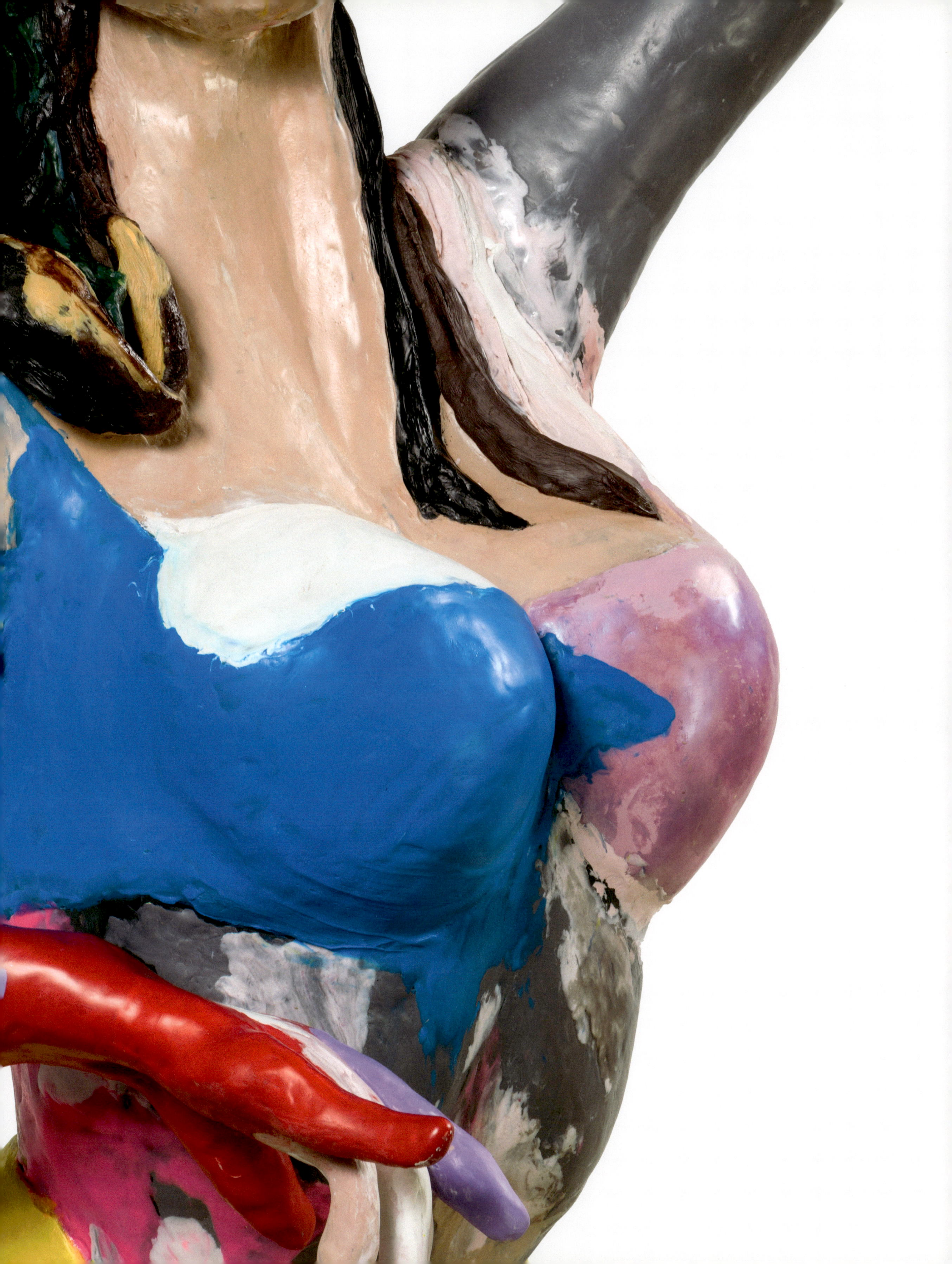

Maquettes

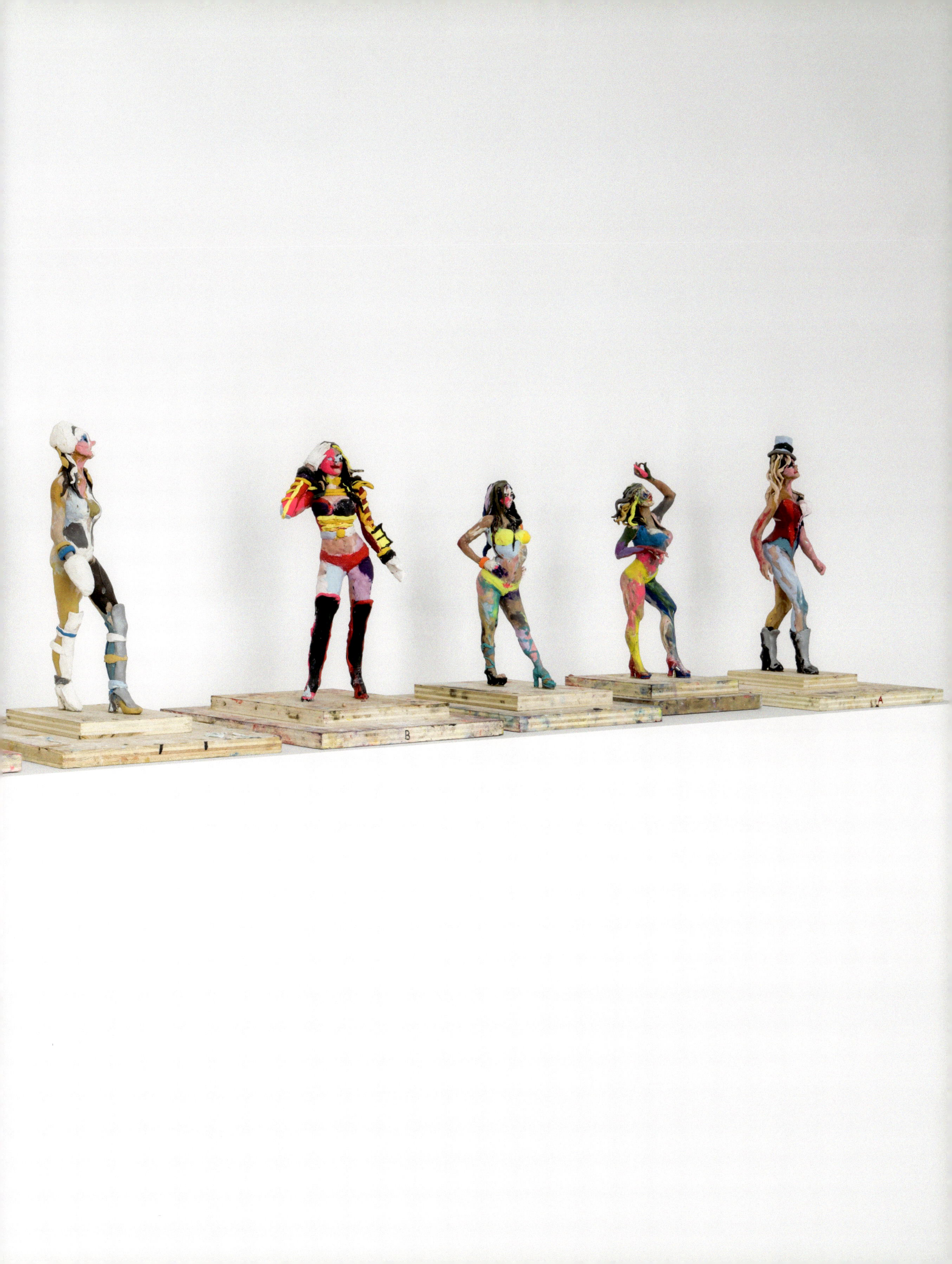
B
A

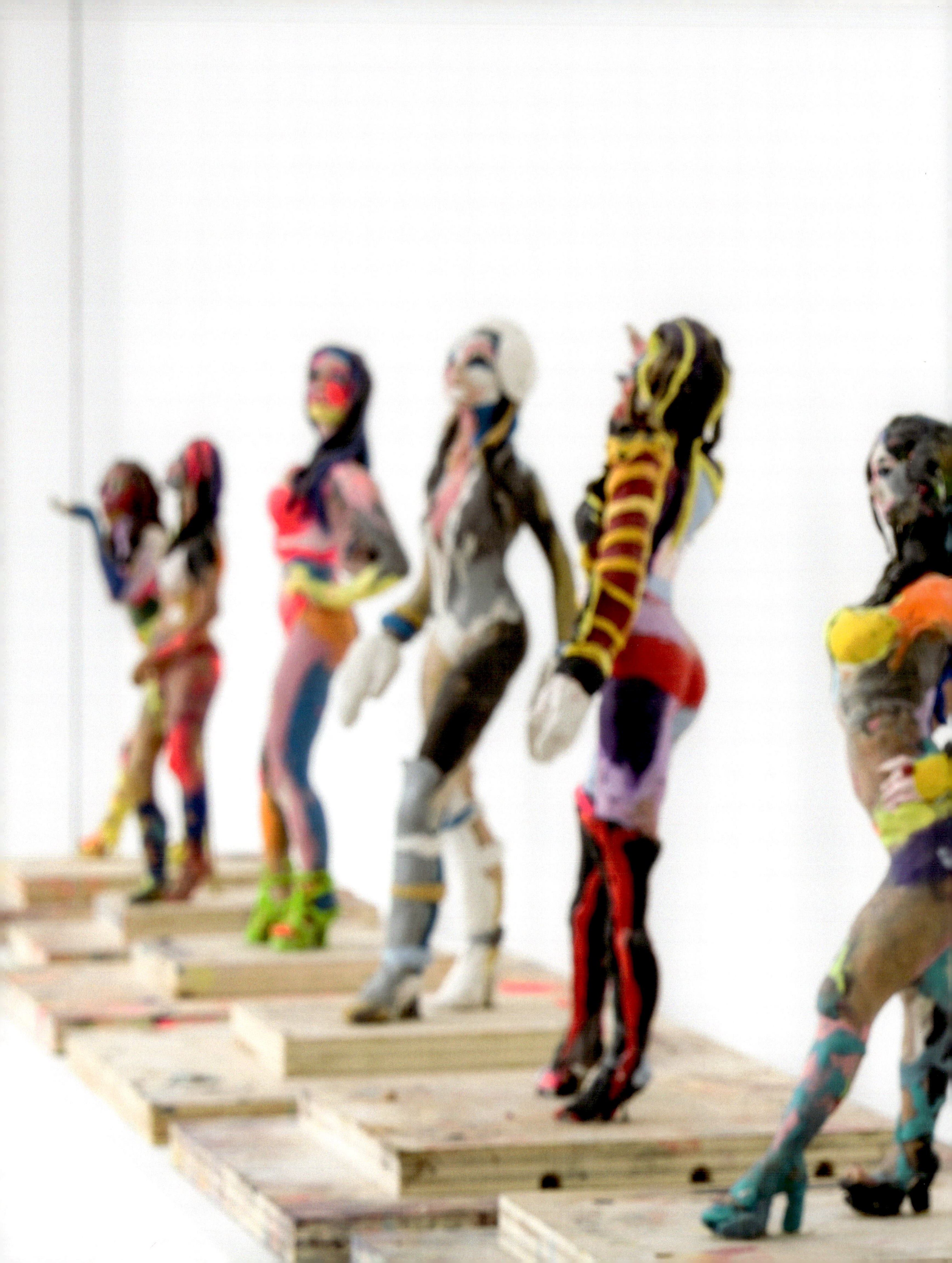

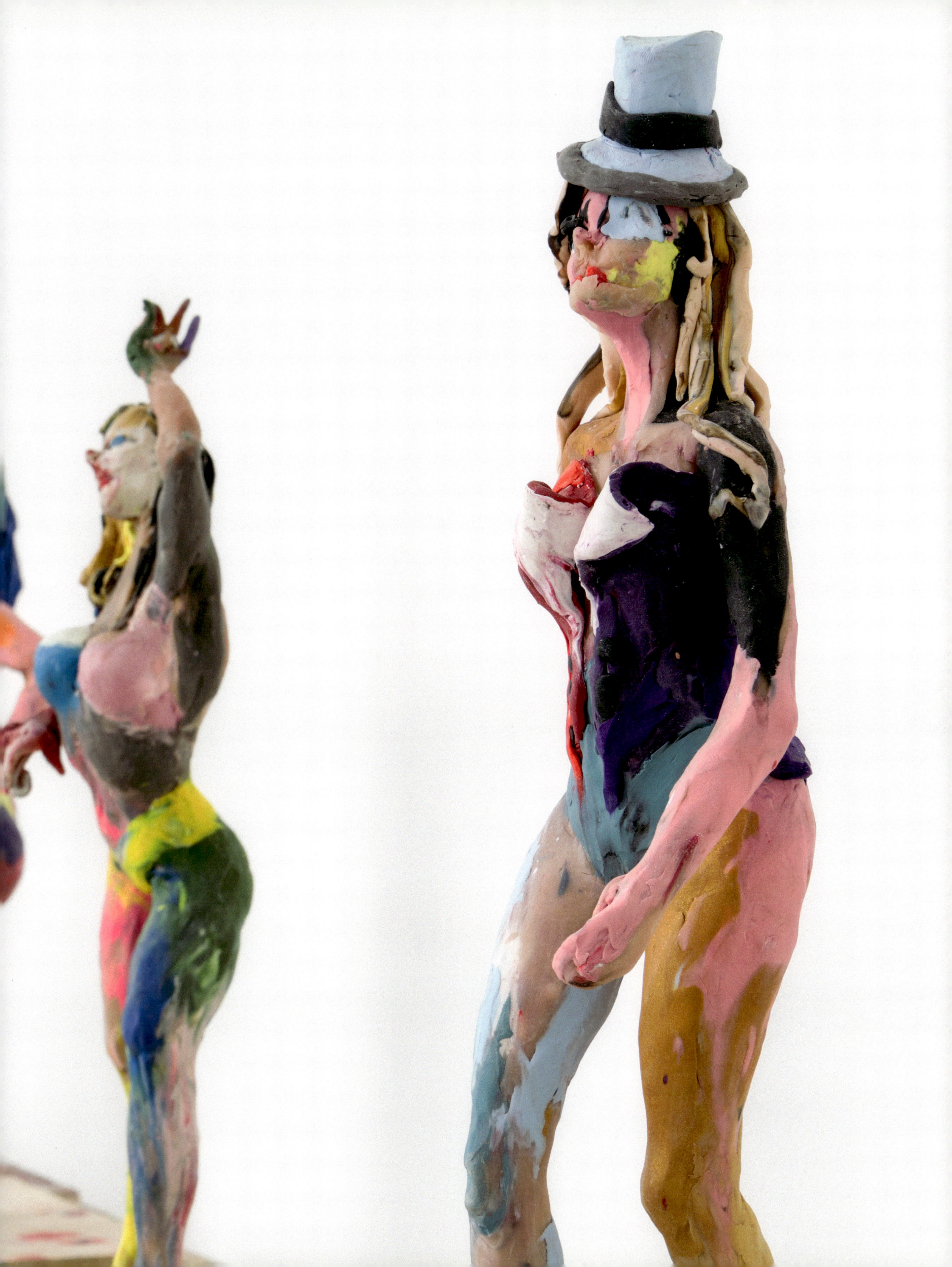

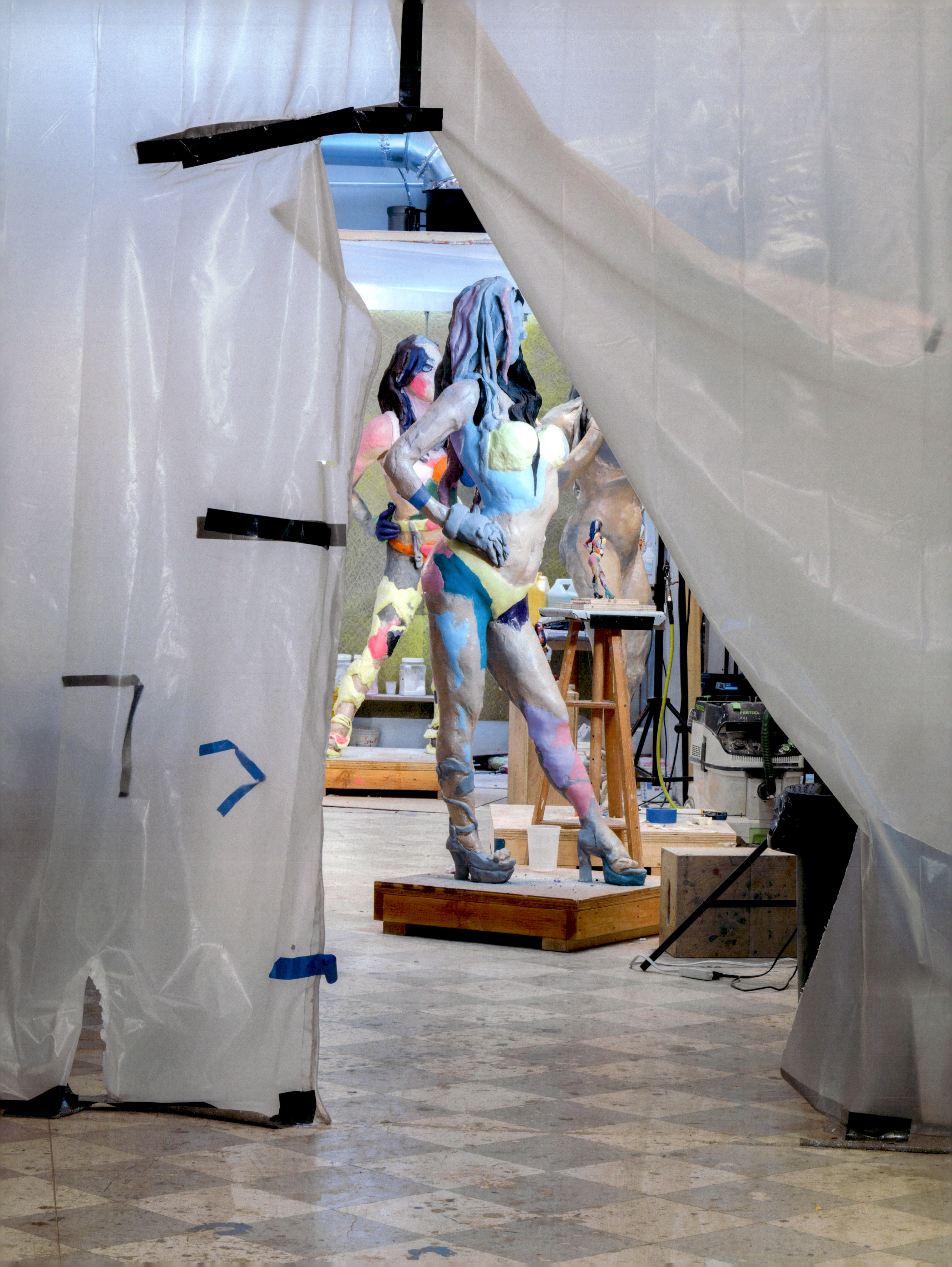
FESTOOL

Secrets

A Conversation between Tom Ford and Rachel Feinstein

Tom Ford: We can talk about all sorts of things. How are you?

Rachel Feinstein: I'm excited, actually. A bunch of interesting stuff is happening. Do you know Chatsworth House [in Derbyshire, England]?

TF: Yes, I stayed there once.

RF: That's right—the Duke and Duchess [of Devonshire] talked about you to me.

TF: We were lucky enough to be there for a weekend but we only had dinner with them once. I think the duchess and I talked a lot about horses.

RF: They liked you.

TF: Isn't it incredible to visit all the white marble sculptures in the gallery by candlelight? Oh my god!

RF: Yes. I've been invited as an artist in residence at Chatsworth to make a permanent work for the house.

TF: So you're moving to Chatsworth?!

RF: Yes, for a bit, with the whole family. [My husband] John [Currin] has never been there.

TF: He has not been there?

RF: No, he didn't come with me on the first trip—I went there alone.

TF: Oh, he's going to love it.

RF: The minute he gets there I know he's not going to want to leave, because when he sees all those old master paintings and drawings up close every night by himself, I swear, I don't think he'll ever be able to get out of there. You know, he likes to stay home more than I do—he's still an Oklahoma boy at heart.

TF: How does he cope with you? You're very much interested in being out and about.

RF: It's true. I grew up with New Yorkers who raised me in Miami. My parents would go to Russia because they were in the mood for caviar—very cosmopolitan [*laughs*].

TF: I met your parents once—your mother was very vivacious and outgoing, and your father was very quiet, but every now and then he would say something very witty. That feels very much like you and John.

RF: That's true—my weaknesses have always been John's strengths. Sometimes I'm very impulsive and John's thing is that everything you do has to matter, and there are no bad paintings of his out there because he's so controlled about it. Being more serious can be a good thing.

TF: Is there anything you've made and released into the world that you wish you hadn't done?

RF: No, I met John when I had just turned twenty-three. He influenced me very early.

TF: Where did you and John meet?

RF: Right after I went to Columbia, I was in a small group show at Exit Art [in New York]. You know, I wrote a thesis paper at Columbia University for my History of Sexuality course that was called "The History of Pubic Hair Styles."

TF: We are in the hairless era and it's so bizarre!

RF: But it says so much about our society. I documented all of the different times in history by using visuals of pubic hair styles, from even the Incas. I found all this crazy stuff in some of my father's medical books. Basically, the historical reason that people would remove their pubic hair was because of vaginal warts, syphilis, and other horrible diseases. They would have to shave everything down there and they would wear merkins because no one liked the way they looked with no hair down there.

TF: Years ago I did a fashion shoot about male nudity for *GQ Style*. I just got ordinary guys and I wanted to discuss the fact that male nudity challenges us in our culture.

Many of these guys had shaved or trimmed their pubic hair, so I had a bunch of merkins made. In the end Conde Nast nixed the whole thing, but yes, I'm very familiar with merkins. And I find the history of pubic hair interesting. What else did you study at Columbia?

RF: I ended up being a religion major there because I wasn't allowed to be an art major. My parents thought that was a dead-end job.

TF: Oh, and you can do so much with a religion degree!

RF: [*Laughs.*] Exactly. I remember reading the book *Purity and Danger* by the social anthropologist Mary Douglas. It was fascinating. It talks about how when the Puritans first came to America they had to live in these dirt hovels with their animals, all sleeping in the same room. They were so freaked out by filth—the strictness of Puritanism and then the witch hunts came about because they couldn't control the filth of the new world.

TF: Well, the Puritan thing is still part of American culture. In fashion, Americans are freaked out by even a little too much style. There's a bland quality inherent to American standards of beauty. Just compare it to the French—it's dramatically different.

RF: These ideas about control, specifically of your body, relate a lot to *Secrets*. But then there's this side of me that always wants to be able to let go and be free. How can you be free in these times? Especially as a woman...

TF: So bring it back to *Secrets*.

RF: When I was in college, I was always making art, but on the side. I was writing my History of Sexuality paper on pubic hair while making these life-size sculptures that were casts of my body on all fours with giant vaginas coming out of my mouth, out of my breasts, and out of my vagina. It was really violent feminist work, around the time when Kiki Smith was starting to make it big.

TF: I did not realize you worked with Kiki Smith.

RF: Yes, she was my teacher at Skowhegan [School of Painting and Sculpture]. She is just an incredibly powerful artist and woman. Judy Pfaff and Ursula von Rydingsvard are also my mentors. They are these amazing, deep, dark, and powerful women—almost like the witches with the Puritans—who molded me early on. And so in my early twenties, I was making this kind of art.

Did you know that I wrote my final paper for religion about "Sleeping Beauty"? Have you ever heard the real story? It's crazy. The Brothers Grimm changed it from the original and then Walt Disney really changed it, but the original story is that the beautiful daughter falls into a deathlike coma from a splinter and the father can't stand his grief so he walls her up in a castle and moves away. Anyway, she's sleeping and after a while the whole kingdom gradually disintegrates into ruins from neglect. The castle gets covered in black thorny vines, which still is part of the "Sleeping Beauty" legacy story. And then a king comes by and hacks his way into the castle and sees this sleeping young woman and rapes her. She doesn't wake up. He goes on his way, and nine months later her body births twins.

TF: Oh my god. You couldn't make that today.

RF: No, definitely not.

TF: You couldn't even make *Lolita* today.

RF: The problem is how it affects artists. It feels like no one's allowed to do anything outside of their sphere.

TF: Oh my god!

RF: So she has a boy and a girl, fraternal twins. They claw themselves up her body and try to suckle from her, and that is when she wakes up. That's the real story.

TF: That's really wild…

RF: The message is not that she wakes up because of a man kissing her. It's that she's only able to "wake up" as a woman when she's able to fully support life and actually be aware of that responsibility. I did research into women giving birth in comas—horribly, the cases on record I referenced were of women who were raped by hospital attendants while in comas and no one noticed that they were pregnant until it was too late. The wild thing is that as long as their bodies are being nourished, women can actually birth children without assistance and without even being awake.

TF: I believe that—it makes total sense.

RF: And the babies can find the breasts by smell and feed themselves and live in this suspended state as long as both the mother and child are getting mutually fed. Isn't that incredible?

TF: That is incredible.

RF: So, based on that story, I made this humping castle—it had a motor underneath that made it move up and down in a sexual way—on top of Sleeping Beauty's bed, where I slept every night for six weeks while people would come into the gallery to watch me, and the weirdest thing is that is when I met John. I became completely confused because I fell in love for the first time and he was almost ten years older than me and more established. So I stopped making that type of work altogether. And *Secrets* is the first time I started making that kind of work again.

TF: When someone looks at your sculpture from *Secrets*, what do you want them to feel? Because for me they are very powerful. They're also slightly vulgar, but there is an enormous beauty in the vulgarity. Am I feeling what you want? I mean, you can't not look at them. They dominate a room.

RF: They do. I'm very proud of them. But it's an interesting question. A very dear old friend who owns my work said to me, "Why can't you make their faces beautiful the way John makes his women beautiful?" And I said, "I think they're beautiful."

TF: I agree, but also your work is impressionistic.

RF: Some people felt that my women look as if they've been beaten up, which surprised me. Everything beautiful is always in the eye of the beholder. And I guess that's where I feel very happy with them. Being a woman who has three children, having given birth three times and completely seeing and feeling the whole thing, I just think that I have an understanding of the blood and guts and the real side of everything. But I also love fantasy and fairy tales and glamour so much too. We've talked before about the idea that a male designer for women is different from a woman designing for other women.

TF: I've often thought about that. There have, of course, been some incredible women designers, like Coco Chanel or Madame Grès, but often I find that many female designers have a hard time letting go of their own built-in insecurities about their bodies. Unfortunately, because of this they are often less free to think about an ideal woman or a woman in general or a woman of our time.

RF: John also thinks that clothes made by women designers are not sexy.

TF: I think that one reason there are so many successful gay male designers is that gay men straddle both sides—we can be a kind of aggressor and we can also understand what it feels like to be submissive. We can identify and relate to what a woman feels. But at the same time, we can remain objective, because we're not women, so we don't have certain preconceived feelings about our bodies as women.

RF: I think that's a beautiful idea actually. I like how you can transport yourself into this fantasy world. I guess I'm trying to do that with these sculptures.

TF: You've mentioned fairy tales and fantasies a few times now.

RF: I'm obsessed with fairy tales and with this idea of the facade that one makes, this perfect shiny fake front, but then there's this dark inner core lurking underneath. Your movies are always just completely about that to me. There's this beautiful presentation but then there's something scary happening quietly behind and you really don't want to go there, but you must. That to me is actually what everything is about in life and art. It's this duality. We are walking through life knowing that we are going to die at any moment and that's it.

TF: Exactly, and there's a fear. And we try to kind of make everything feel normal through a facade. Our whole culture is built on that. We find it actually a bit embarrassing to die. We have a total denial of death. We feel that if we can control everything and look pretty, then we don't have to think about the fact that from birth to death we're just killing time.

RF: That's been my complaint about the contemporary art world. Before, there was an absolute embrace of this dark side and death, this sinister decay—think of Dürer or Hans Baldung. That just does not exist in the same way in contemporary art at the moment. Collectors don't want to think about their own bodies' demise; it's not at all sexy or glamorous, and it doesn't make them feel good about themselves, so they just don't want to see it in their house. Being from a family with a medical background, I've realized you might as well show that side as well—it's life.

TF: Well, art is now as marketed as fashion, and it's all just a mirror of our culture and our values.

RF: When I first got out of college in '93, the art world was a very small place. Everybody knew everybody. It was very formal and stiff and there was absolutely no glamour—it was frowned upon. There was definitely no association with the fashion world. I remember there was a big article in the *New York Times* Styles section in 1999 that mentioned me. It was called "The Artist Is a Glamour Puss" and it was about how pretty young women artists were wearing designer clothes to openings for the first time ever. And then Roberta Smith wrote her attack. So it's amazing that now the topic of pretty women artists liking fashion has all been pushed away. You can go to the Met Ball [the Costume Institute Gala held by New York's Metropolitan Museum of Art] as an artist and wear the big gowns and nobody says anything about it looking bad for your career. But in the early stages it was seen as very bad, and truthfully, I paid my dues.

As an interesting correlation, I was recently thinking about how throughout history there have always been different creative fields that join together during specific periods. For example, the Ballets Russes combined artists and musicians of their day like Picasso and Stravinsky. Many people just don't have the attention spans for a three-hour opera or a ballet anymore, but they can sit through a five-minute fashion show or walk in and out of a museum or gallery show, so now it's the union of art and fashion for a reason: our current screen-addicted brains.

TF: Well, I'm afraid that I don't have the attention span for it most of the time. We're not used to watching something from one angle anymore. When you sit through a play, you're just literally watching something from the same vantage point for two hours, but we've become accustomed to a cut every three or four seconds for a different shot, a different angle. Live performances can be dull by comparison. But then, of course, they can also be visceral and electric in a way that a filmed performance can rarely be.

TF: Out of all the works you've made, which one makes you the most excited and why?

RF: That's a very good question. The *Secrets* excite me most right now because they bring me back full circle to my youth again and that feeling. What I miss about being young is this idea that you could jump right in and then figure out whether it was a mistake later. And as you get older you're more afraid of making mistakes and you think a bit too much. I had so much crazy, boundless, violent young energy. I think these sculptures portray that and it makes me very happy.

TF: They definitely have enormous energy.

RF: And after all these years I've learned a lot, so now I also can make them with a higher level of craft.

TF: How are they made?

RF: Actually this is something that took me a really long time to figure out. First, I made the little ones from Sculpey, a bake-in-your-oven colorful children's polymer clay. I tried to carve the larger ones in foam, using the maquettes as inspiration, and it totally didn't work. When I'm going from small to big, as long as it's kind of abstract, I can play with it. But if it's figurative, I start to self-correct the problems of the small ones. So if the arm is a little bit too long on the small one, I'll fix it on the big one and it will lose that raw, animalistic energy. I found the atelier of Seward Johnson, who developed the 3-D imaging technology that we used, and they do different types of laser 3-D scanning. It can capture every little bump and detail in the model and then use a robot to carve the figures to any scale out of foam. I have the large versions made a little thinner so that we can then add the layers of different transparent and solid colors on top.

TF: So those big ones are carved out of foam?

RF: They're made out of a high-density foam that is actually weatherproof for outdoors, but we don't display them outdoors.

TF: Did you coat them in resin or anything?

RF: Each of those colors is a hand-applied pigmented resin. We would color-match the little sculptures and make piles of putty that would cure in one hour to three hours. It comes out a little like chewing gum. Then we'd apply it by hand. There are two different types of resins.

TF: It's very cool that you made them look like they are made of Play-Doh.

RF: Yes, of course there's that famous Jeff Koons Play-Doh sculpture, but he made it in painted metal instead of pigmented resins. I think he wanted it to be more archival by making it out of metal, but it's almost impossible to mimic the way colors really mix together in clay by using paint. Right now I'm also working with the Nymphenburg factory in Munich, who did the pedestals for me, to think about making outdoor versions of the *Secrets* using glazed ceramic. I'm very excited about that.

TF: Full scale?

RF: Yes. That's one of the options that we're looking at for Chatsworth, possibly doing some of *Secrets* for their outdoor garden. It's a weird take on classical sculpture, to have these kind of monster women in your garden.

TF: You should make them all in white and place them in the room you go through by candlelight.

RF: I love that idea!

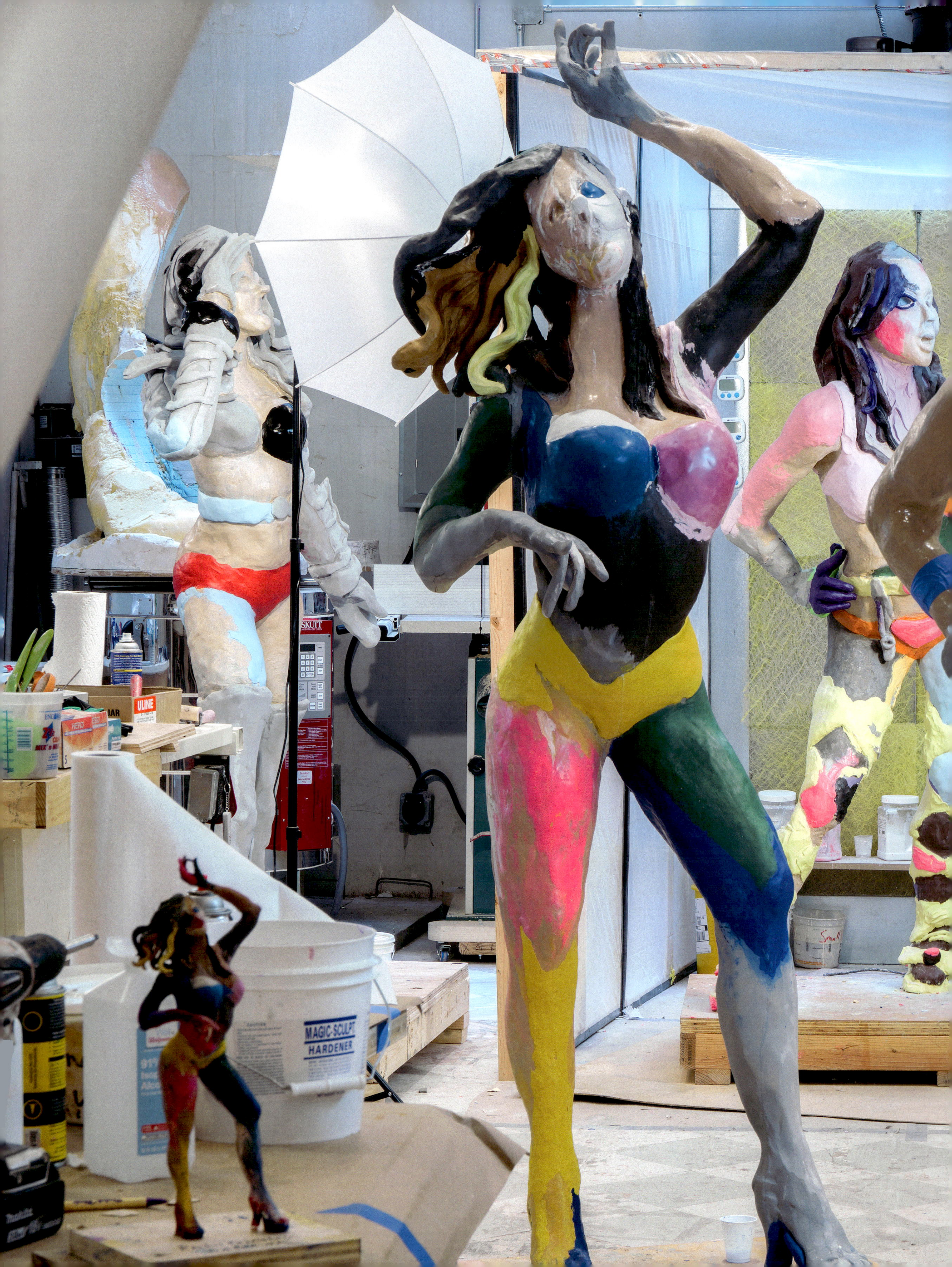
ULINE
MAGIC-SCULPT
HARDENER

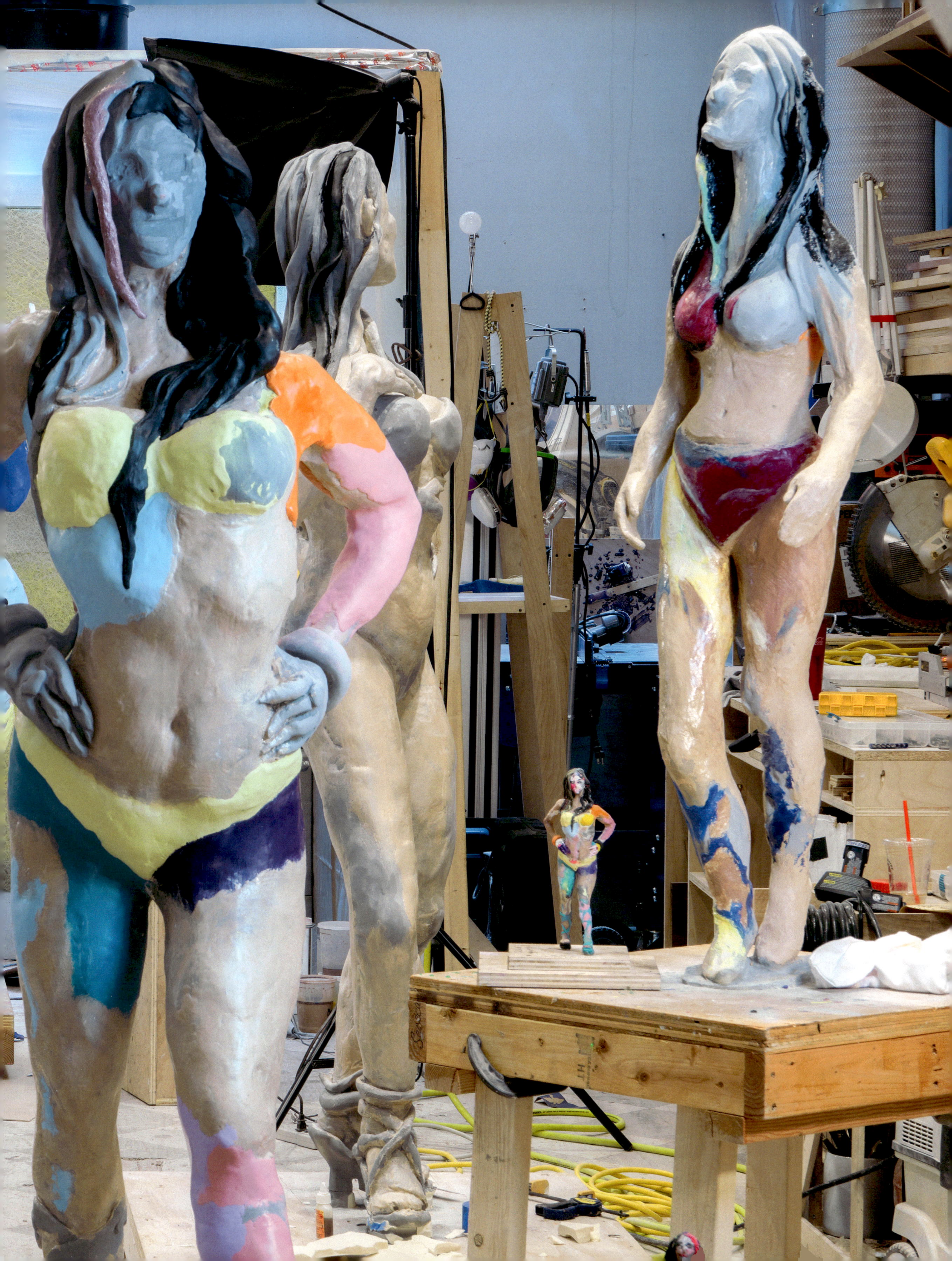

List of Works

Ballerina, 2018
Hand-applied colored resin over foam
with wooden base
85 ½ × 31 × 27 inches
(217.2 × 78.7 × 68.6 cm)
p. 69

Ballerina Maquette, 2017
Polymer clay and wire
11 ½ × 4 ¼ × 4 ¼ inches
(29.2 × 10.8 × 10.8 cm)
pp. 74–75

Bandleader, 2018
Hand-applied colored resin over foam
with wooden base
76 × 40 × 30 inches
(193 × 101.6 × 76.2 cm)
p. 33

Bandleader Maquette, 2017
Polymer clay and wire
12 ¼ × 6 ½ × 6 ½ inches
(31.1 × 16.5 × 16.5 cm)
pp. 74–75

Butterfly, 2018
Hand-applied colored resin over foam
with wooden base
78 ½ × 37 × 32 ½ inches
(199.4 × 94 × 82.6 cm)
p. 7

Butterfly Maquette, 2017
Polymer clay and wire
10 ½ × 4 ¼ × 4 ¼ inches
(26.7 × 10.8 × 10.8 cm)
pp. 74–75

Feathers, 2018
Hand-applied colored resin over foam
with wooden base
77 × 37 ½ × 29 ½ inches
(195.6 × 95.3 × 74.9 cm)
p. 15

Feathers Maquette, 2017
Polymer clay and wire
12 ½ × 5 × 5 inches
(31.8 × 12.7 × 12.7 cm)
pp. 74–75

Fireworks, 2018
Hand-applied colored resin over foam
with wooden base
77 × 29 × 28 inches
(195.6 × 73.7 × 71.1 cm)
p. 53

Fireworks Maquette, 2017
Polymer clay and wire
10 ½ × 4 ¼ × 4 ¼ inches
(26.7 × 10.8 × 10.8 cm)
pp. 74–75

Icicles, 2018
Hand-applied colored resin over foam
with wooden base
57 × 18 ½ × 20 inches
(144.8 × 47 × 50.8 cm)
p. 43

Icicles Maquette, 2017
Polymer clay and wire
12 ⅝ × 4 ¾ × 4 ¾ inches
(32.1 × 12.1 × 12.1 cm)
pp. 74–75

Spats, 2018
Hand-applied colored resin over foam
with wooden base
57 × 17 × 19 inches
(144.8 × 43.2 × 48.3 cm)
p. 63

Spats Maquette, 2017
Polymer clay and wire
13 ⅜ × 4 ¼ × 4 ¼ inches
(34 × 10.8 × 10.8 cm)
pp. 74–75

Tourist, 2018
Hand-applied colored resin over foam
with wooden base
57 × 17 × 14 ½ inches
(144.8 × 43.2 × 36.8 cm)
p. 25

Tourist Maquette, 2017
Polymer clay and wire
10 ½ × 3 ½ × 3 ½ inches
(26.7 × 8.9 × 8.9 cm)
pp. 74–75

Published on the occasion of the exhibition

Rachel Feinstein
Secrets

January 11–February 17, 2018

Gagosian Beverly Hills
456 North Camden Drive
Beverly Hills, CA 90210
+1 310 271 9400
www.gagosian.com

Publication © 2019 Gagosian

All artwork © Rachel Feinstein

"Secrets" © Rachel Feinstein and Tom Ford

Director: Rebecca Sternthal
Gagosian exhibition coordinators: Madeline Amos, Dean Anes, Ronnie Gunter, Jacqueline Hulburd, Hannah Kauffman, Melissa Lazarov, Deborah M. McLeod, Courtney Raterman, Amanda Stoffel, and Sarah Womble

Director of Publications: Alison McDonald
Editor: Priya Bhatnagar
Publication coordinator: David Arkin
Copy editor: Polly Watson

Design by Goto Design, New York
Color separations by Artproduct, Los Angeles
Printed by Pureprint Group, Uckfield, England

All photographs by Jeff McLane, with the exception of the following: pp. 1, 4–5, 12–13, 22–23, 30–31, 40–41, 50–51, 60–61, 66–67, 74 (lettering), 78, 79, 88–89, 91, and endpapers: Rob McKeever.

All rights reserved. No part of this publication may be reprinted or reproduced in any form or by any electronic, mechanical, or other means, now known or hereafter invented, including photocopying and recording, or in any information retrieval system, without prior written permission from the copyright holders.

ISBN 978-1-938748-71-4

Rachel Feinstein would like to thank the following individuals for their contributions to this exhibition and book:

Tom Ford, for the most interesting interview ever

Takaya Goto and Lesley Chi
for their thoughtful book design

My studio team: Carlos Vela-Prado, Dmitri Hertz, Collin Willis, Cara Chan, Michael Sims, Owen Landers, and Liz Lessner

Jon Lash at Digital Atelier

Louis Yoh and Sam Kirby Yoh
for alcohol/music/support

Lisa Yuskavage and Sarah Sze
for studio visits and inspiration

Rebecca Sternthal, Deborah M. McLeod, Dean Anes, Amanda Stoffel, Jacque Hulburd, Alison McDonald, and Priya Bhatnagar at Gagosian for everything!

Larry Gagosian, Chrissie Erpf, and Melissa Lazarov
for the love and support they have always shown me

John, Francis, Hollis, and Flora Currin
for all their love

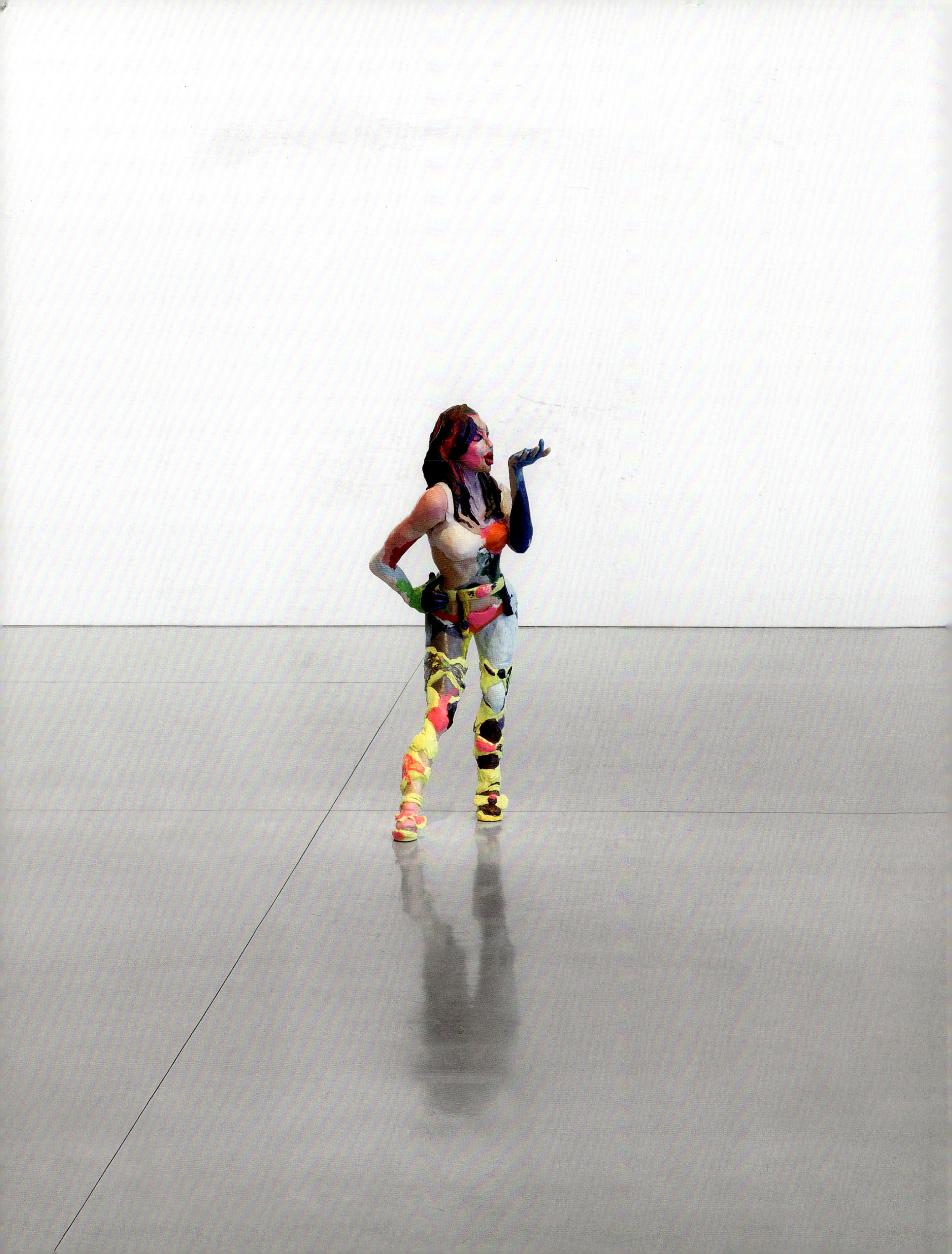